MAGIC MADE EASY

First published in the UK in 2011 by
QED Publishing
A Quarto Group Company
230 City Road
London EC1V 2TT

www.qed-publishing.co.uk

Library of Congress Control Numbers:
2008010182
2008010183
2008010190
2008010191

ISBN 978 1 84835 810 2

Printed in China

Editor Michael Downey
Designer Louise Downey
Illustrator Mark Turner for Beehive Illustrations

Picture credits
Anikó Ungár 101
Corbis: Lawrence Manning 45, Bettmann/CORBIS 104
Getty Images: Hulton Archive 14 and 25, Adam Gault 59, Domino 71, Al Francekevich 77, 95, Barcroft Media via Getty Images 99
Rex Features: ITV 13, FreemantleMedia Ltd 17, ITV 30, Willi Schneider 35
Shutterstock: Andrejs Pidjass 43, 3dfoto 49, spiller 61, Ilya Andriyanov 67, Feng Yu 73, TV Times/Scope Features.com 75, Berislav Kovacevic 109
Michael Vincent 57

MAGIC MADE EASY

JON TREMAINE

QED Publishing

Contents

Contents

How to use this book

A disappearing pencil, paper clips that mysteriously join together, a banknote that spins around all by itself, a matchstick that jumps about in your hand – these are fun tricks to do with simple props you can carry in your pocket. Tricks don't have to be complicated to be impressive!

(2) **Difficulty rating**

The tricks get harder throughout the book, so each trick has been given a rating. Two is the easiest and seven is the hardest. The most difficult tricks will take a bit of practice to get right, but the results will be worth it!

(1) **Preparation**

Sometimes you will need to prepare something in advance to make a trick work.

Up your sleeve

Now you see it, now you don't! The vanishing key trick is a real 'fooler'.

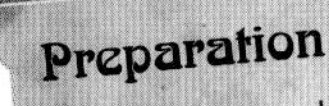

(1) **Preparation**

- Attach one end of the elastic cord to the key and the other end to the safety pin.
- Fix the safety pin to the inside of your jacket's right sleeve at the top.
- Allow the key and elastic to slide down inside the sleeve. Adjust the length of the elastic so that the key hangs about three centimetres up from the end of the sleeve. Put the jacket on.

1 Just before you do this trick, reach inside your sleeve and pull the key down and grip it between your right thumb and first finger. Once you are sure that the elastic is hidden by the back of your hand, let your audience see the key.

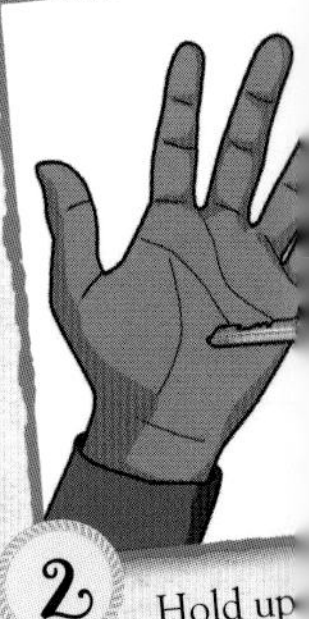

2 Hold up ... that it is fa... audience s... palm with...

34

Playing to the crowd

To be a good magician, you must practise your acting skills. This is because magic is as much about your performance as it is about the tricks. Always try to get your audience involved as much as possible. For example, when you do a money trick, borrow some coins or a banknote from someone in the audience.

3 Props needed...

Each page will tell you the props you to need in order to perform the trick. You should be able to find most of these objects around your home.

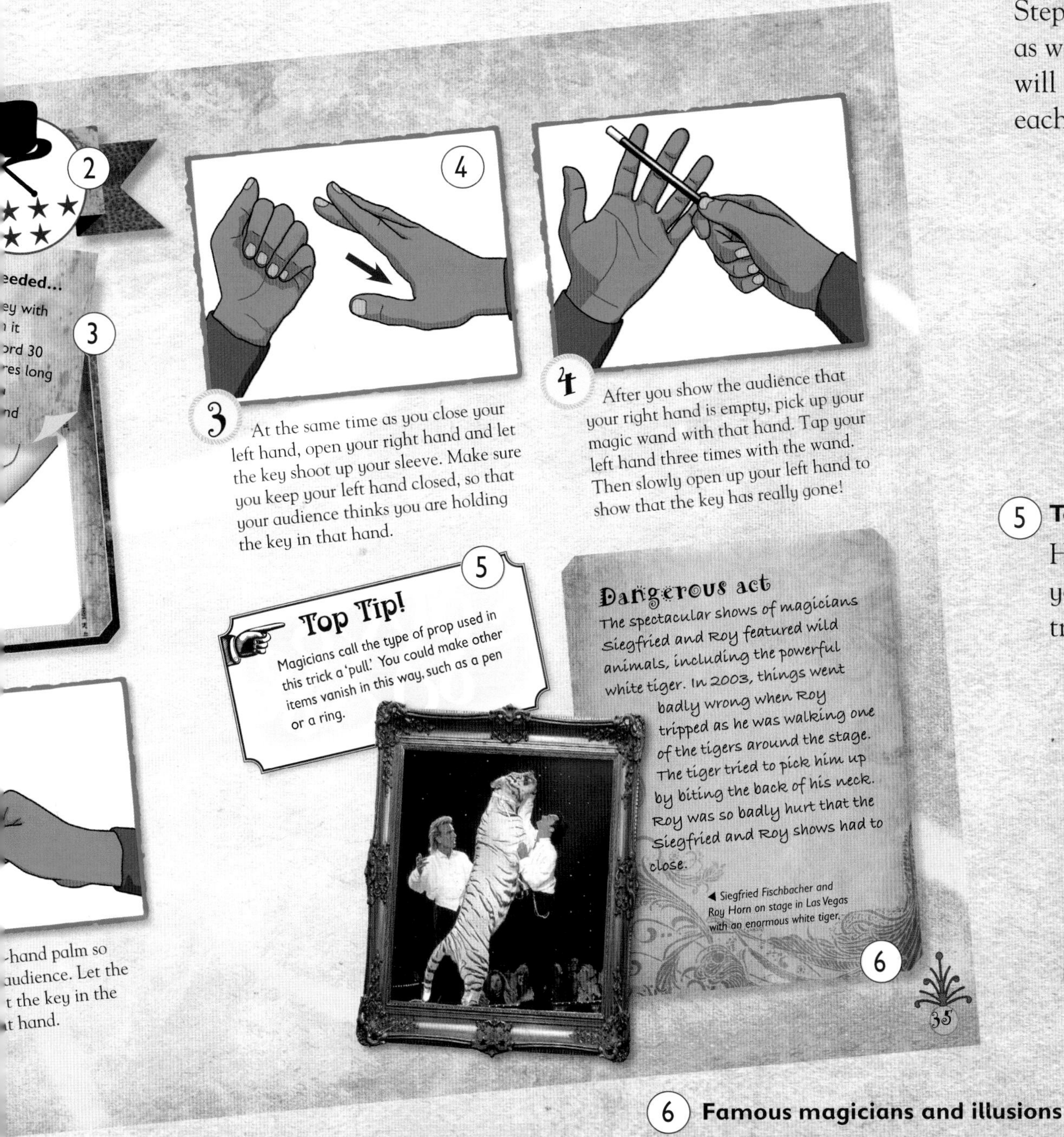

3 At the same time as you close your left hand, open your right hand and let the key shoot up your sleeve. Make sure you keep your left hand closed, so that your audience thinks you are holding the key in that hand.

4 After you show the audience that your right hand is empty, pick up your magic wand with that hand. Tap your left hand three times with the wand. Then slowly open up your left hand to show that the key has really gone!

Top Tip!

Magicians call the type of prop used in this trick a 'pull.' You could make other items vanish in this way, such as a pen or a ring.

Dangerous act

The spectacular shows of magicians Siegfried and Roy featured wild animals, including the powerful white tiger. In 2003, things went badly wrong when Roy tripped as he was walking one of the tigers around the stage. The tiger tried to pick him up by biting the back of his neck. Roy was so badly hurt that the Siegfried and Roy shows had to close.

◄ Siegfried Fischbacher and Roy Horn on stage in Las Vegas with an enormous white tiger.

35

4 Stages and illustrations

Step-by-step instructions, as well as illustrations, will guide you through each trick.

5 Top Tip!

Hints and tips help you to perform the tricks better!

6 Famous magicians and illusions

Find out who are the most exciting and skilful magicians, and what amazing feats they have performed.

Props you'll need

Pocket Tricks

- Banknote
- Cardboard
- Coins
- Crusty bread roll
- Elastic cord
- Envelope
- Glue
- Golf tee
- Handkerchief
- Magic wand
- Matchsticks
- Metal key
- Paper
- Paper clips
- Pen
- Pencil
- Ring
- Safety pin
- Scissors
- Sticky putty
- String

Magical Illusions

- Bangles
- Book
- Coins
- Dictionary
- Glue
- Handkerchief
- Hobby knife
- Jacket with pockets
- Magic wand
- Pack of playing cards
- Paper
- Paper bag
- Pencil
- Red shoelace
- Safety pins
- Scissors
- Straw
- String
- Thimble
- White card
- Yellow shoelace

Paper Tricks

- Banknotes
- Cardboard
- Coins
- Colour magazine
- Coloured sticky tape
- Coloured tissue paper
- Envelopes
- Glue
- Magic wand
- Newspaper
- Paper bags
- Pencils
- Plain postcards
- Pretend banknotes
- Rubber cement
- Ruler
- Scissors
- Sticky tape
- Talcum powder
- White and coloured paper
- Writing paper

Magic with Numbers

- Battery
- Bracelet
- Button
- Cardboard
- Cardboard box
- Chewing gum
- Coins
- Dice
- Domino set
- Envelopes
- Glass bowl
- Key
- Marker pen
- Matchstick
- Paper
- Pencil
- Playing cards
- Pocket calculator
- Ring
- Safety pin
- Scissors
- Small notebook
- Sticky tape

POCKET TRICKS

Vanishing pencil

Make a pencil disappear right through your hand. Don't worry, it doesn't hurt! Your friend will not have a clue how you did it.

Props needed...

* Pencil. If possible, borrow one from your friend

1 Stand with your friend to your left and hold out the palm of your left hand. Grip the pencil in your right hand in the writing position.

2 Tell your friend that you will make the pencil pass right through the palm of your left hand.

3 Bend your right arm at the elbow and swing the pencil up until it is level with your right ear. Bring the pencil down again and gently press the pointed end into your left palm. As you do this, count, "One."

4

Swing the pencil up to your right ear again, and then down into your palm as you count, "Two."

5

Swing the pencil up to your ear a third time. This time, however, slide it behind your ear and leave it there. Bring your empty right hand down to your palm again as if you were still holding the pencil. Press your fingers into your left palm and count, "Three."

6

Show your friend that your hands are empty. The pencil has disappeared!

Top Tip!

This trick works because you keep your friend's attention on your hand. The pencil is only out of sight for a second, which is long enough for you to work your magic.

Magic paper clips

★★

Take two simple paper clips, clip them to a banknote and then magically link them together in the blink of an eye.

Props needed...
- ✶ Two paper clips
- ✶ Banknote. You can also use a piece of paper the same size as a banknote

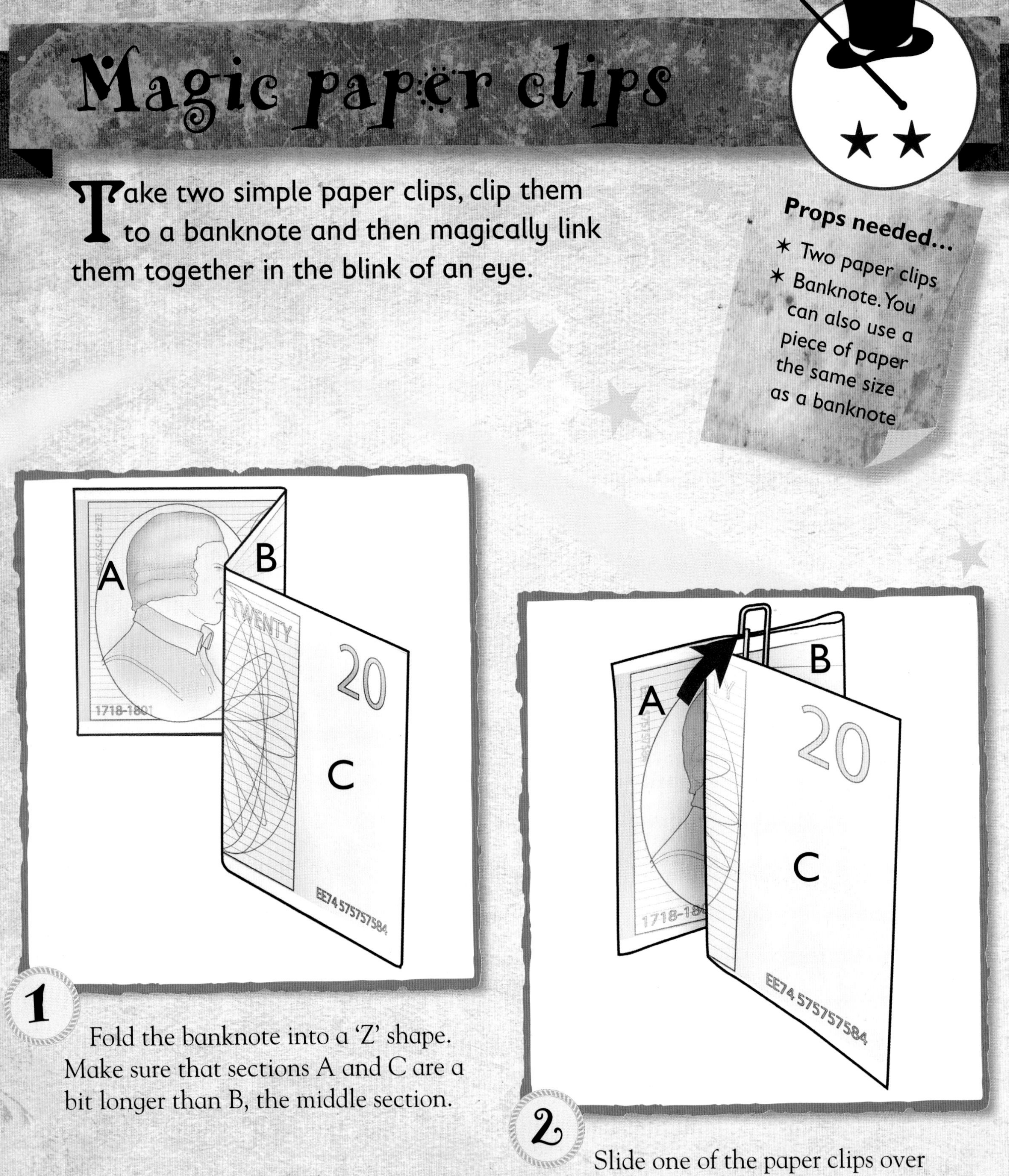

1 Fold the banknote into a 'Z' shape. Make sure that sections A and C are a bit longer than B, the middle section.

2 Slide one of the paper clips over sections A and B. Look at the drawing to make sure that you get this right.

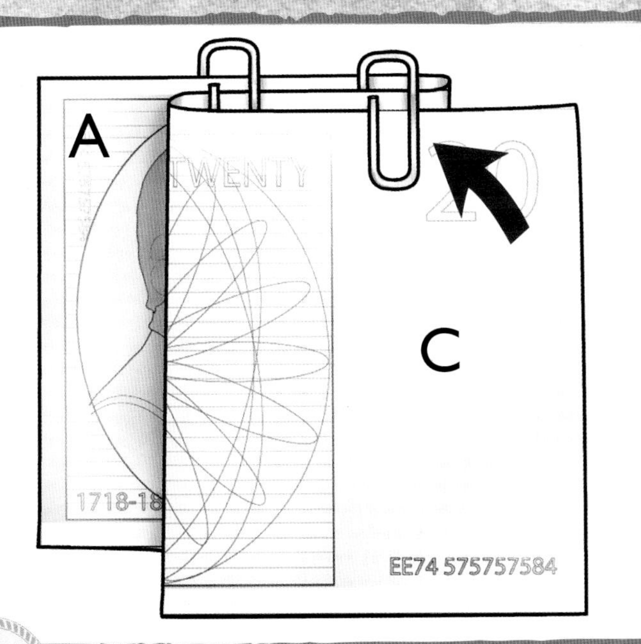

3

Now slide the second paper clip over sections B and C of the banknote.

4

Hold the end of section A in your left hand and the end of section C in your right hand. Pull these two apart with a quick, sharp pull. The two clips will link together and fly into the air.

Top Tip!

Why not make up a story and tell it to your friend while you do the trick? It could be about a boy and a girl who meet, fall in love and get married.

Funniest magician

Many people would agree that Tommy Cooper (1921–1984) was one of the funniest magicians ever. He was famous for wearing a fez – a red felt hat with a tassel. His tricks nearly always went wrong, and the audience laughed when he tried to put things right. He did one of his funniest tricks wearing a red cloak. From this, he pulled out lots of things, including a bucket, a beer crate and a step-ladder!

◀ *With his fez, his enormous feet and his silly laugh, Tommy Cooper always made his audience laugh – whether his magic tricks worked or not!*

Cash in hand

You may not believe that you could get away with this simple, cheeky trick! All you have to do is make a coin vanish in your hand.

Props needed...

* Six coins

Sin Sala Bim

Harry August Jansen (1883–1955), or 'Dante' as he called himself, became a full-time magician when he was just 16 years old. During a show he always said, "Sin Sala Bim" to his audience when they applauded him. No-one knows what this meant! In his most famous illusion, he pretended to saw a woman in half.

▼ *Dante was one of the most gifted magicians of all time. He had a great talent for inventing magic tricks.*

1 With the six coins in your right jacket pocket, say to your audience, "I will need a coin for this trick." Take all the coins out of your jacket pocket and put them on your right-hand palm.

2 With your left first finger, push one of the coins forwards a little and say, "This one will do."

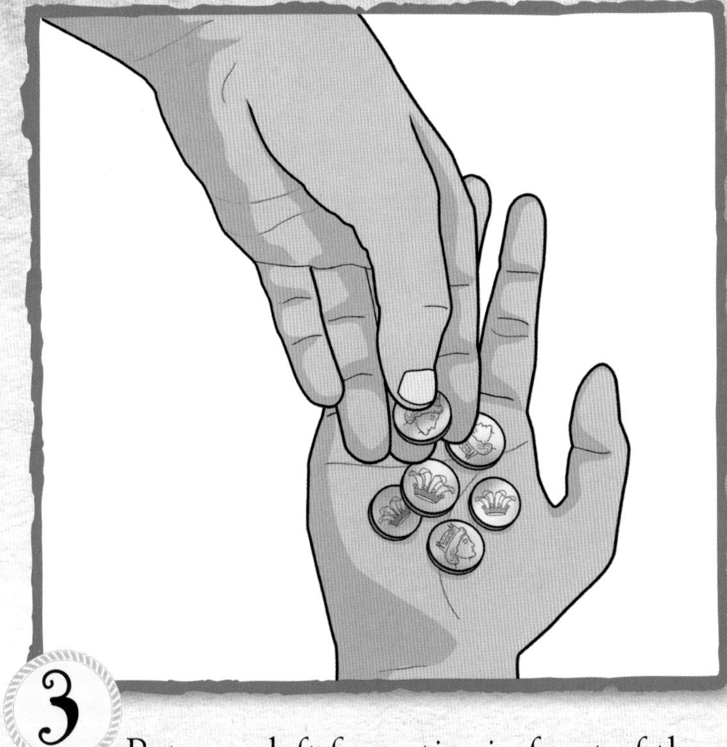

3

Put your left fingertips in front of the coin facing the audience. Your thumb is behind. Make a grabbing action as if you are picking up the coin, but do not take it away. Instead, let it drop back with the other coins.

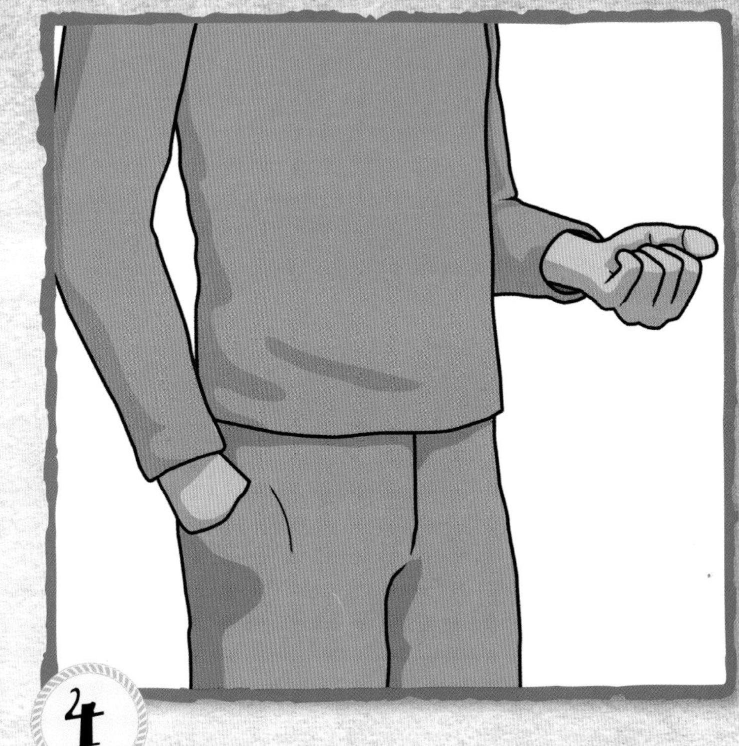

4

Take your left hand away and close it as if it holds the coin. At the same time, put the coins in your right hand back into your pocket. When you take your hand out again, show your audience that it is empty.

5

Of course, your left hand is also empty. Your audience thinks that you have a coin in your left hand, so you must pretend to believe it too. After about five seconds, slowly open your fingers to show your audience that the coin has really disappeared!

Top Tip!

At the end of the trick, make sure that you show your audience both of your hands. They will see that they are empty.

The penny drops

Drop a coin to the ground and make it disappear! To make your audience believe that it has really vanished, you will have to practise your acting skills.

Props needed...

* Coin, which may be borrowed

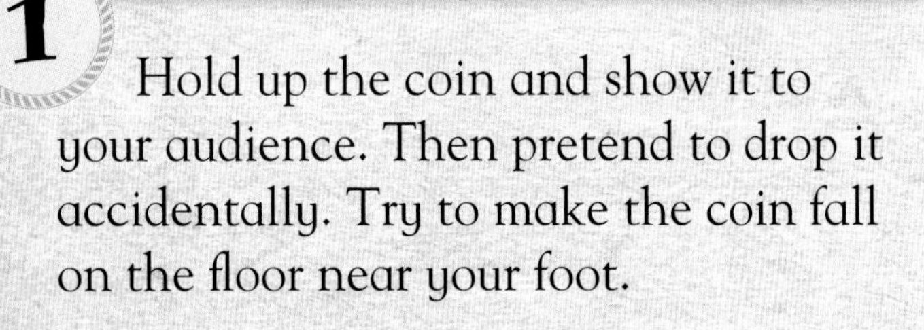

1 Hold up the coin and show it to your audience. Then pretend to drop it accidentally. Try to make the coin fall on the floor near your foot.

2 Everyone will be laughing at your clumsiness. Bend down to pick up the coin, apologizing for dropping it.

Top Tip!

If you are wearing long trousers with turnups, you could drop the coin into one of the turnups as you straighten up, rather than flipping it beneath your shoe.

3

However, instead of picking up the coin, quickly slide it under your shoe with your fingertips.

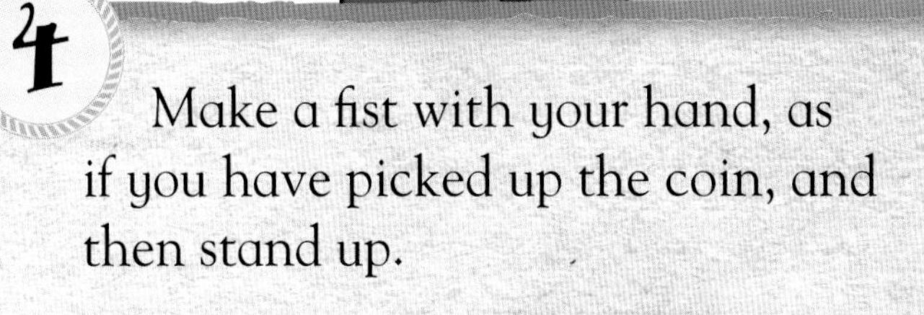

4

Make a fist with your hand, as if you have picked up the coin, and then stand up.

5

Now, you only have to open your hand and show the audience that the coin has really vanished. You should pretend to be as puzzled as your audience when you can't find the coin!

Disappearing elephant

Paul Daniels is one of the world's most successful magicians. He performs small, close-up tricks as well as huge magic illusions in the open air. These include making an elephant vanish! His wife, Debbie McGee, assists him in all his shows. He often saws her in half, makes her float in the air, and causes her to disappear from inside locked boxes.

◀ *Paul Daniels's most famous catchphrase is "You'll like this – not a lot, but you'll like it."*

Money know-how

Your friend will think you have special powers when you predict which coin they will choose.

Props needed...

* Four coins of different values
* Envelope
* Card that fits in the envelope
* Pen
* Glue
* Paper
* Scissors

Preparation

To show you how to do this trick, 5p, 10p, 20p and 50p coins have been used. You can use any other four coins, but remember to change the wording on the labels.

• On the front of the envelope, write, 'You will think of the 10p'.

Point to a coin

• Take the card and, on one side, write, 'Point to a coin'.

You will think of the 5p

• On the other side of the card, write, 'You will think of the 5p'.

You will think of this coin

• On a round label, write, 'You will think of this coin'. Glue this to the 50p coin.

You will think of the 20p

• Now cut out a long, thin label and write on it, 'You will think of the 20p'. Glue this label to one side of the pen.

• Place the coins on the card with the message below facing up. The label on the 50p coin should be facing down. Slide the card into the envelope, which should be face down on the table. Put the pen on the table so that its message is also hidden.

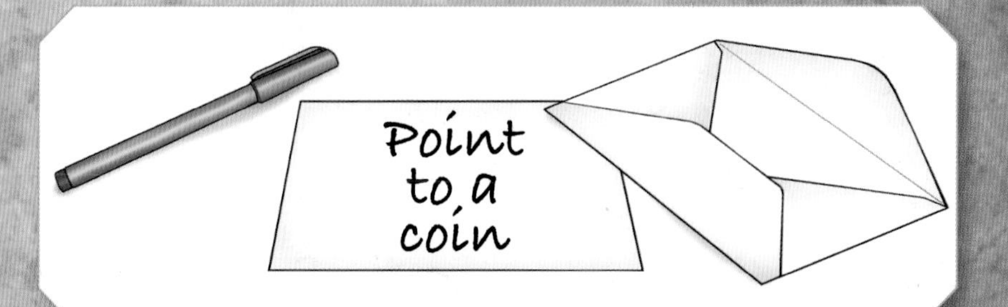

Point to a coin

1 Take the card out of the envelope and put it on the table so that the 'Point to a coin' message is showing.

Point to a coin

2 Slide the coins out of the envelope and arrange them on top of the card. Be careful that your friend doesn't see the label glued to the 50p coin.

3 Pick up the pen, making sure you keep the label hidden. Then say, "I want you to point to one of these coins. I already know which one you will choose. I'm thinking about it and will send you a thought message so that you choose the same one."

4 You can end this trick in one of four different ways, depending on which coin your friend chooses.

1. If the 5p coin is chosen, slide the coins off and turn over the card. The message is 'You will think of the 5p'.

2. If the 10p coin is chosen, ask your friend to turn over the envelope. The message is 'You will think of the 10p'.

3. If the 20p coin is chosen, give your friend the pen to read the message 'You will think of the 20p'. Put the coins and card back into the envelope.

4. If the 50p coin is chosen, ask your friend to turn over the other coins. Then ask them to turn over the 50p with the message 'You will think of this coin'.

Ghostly banknote

Borrow a banknote from your friend and make it spin around in your hands. How is it done? Simple! All you need is a golf tee and some putty.

Props needed...

* Banknote
* Sticky putty
* Golf tee
* Scissors

Preparation

- Ask an adult to cut off the pointed end of the golf tee with scissors to leave about 1.5 centimetres.
- Fill the hollow of the tee with the sticky putty.

1 Grip the tee between the first and second fingers of your right hand. Cover the putty with your thumb. Make sure that you keep the tee hidden from your friend at all times.

2 Take your friend's banknote in your left hand and place it in your right hand. The centre of the banknote should cover the putty. Press with your right thumb so that the tee sticks to the centre of the underside of the banknote.

3 Lift off the banknote with your left hand – it should have the tee stuck to its underside.

4 Lay the note across your palms so that the tee is gripped between the edges of your palms.

Hold the tee between your palms

Top Tip!

Finish the trick by handing the banknote back to your friend. Put the hidden tee into your pocket when your friend is not looking.

5 Keeping a gentle grip on the tee, move one of your hands slightly forward and backward. The note will begin to turn in a mysterious way. Very little movement is needed to make the banknote spin.

Magic matchstick

Watch your friend's amazed expression when you mend a broken matchstick using nothing more than a handkerchief.

Props needed...

* Handkerchief with a wide hem
* Two matchsticks

Preparation

- Look for an open corner of the handkerchief.
- Slide a matchstick into the corner until it is out of sight.

1 Lay the handkerchief on the table. The corner with the hidden matchstick should be closest to you.

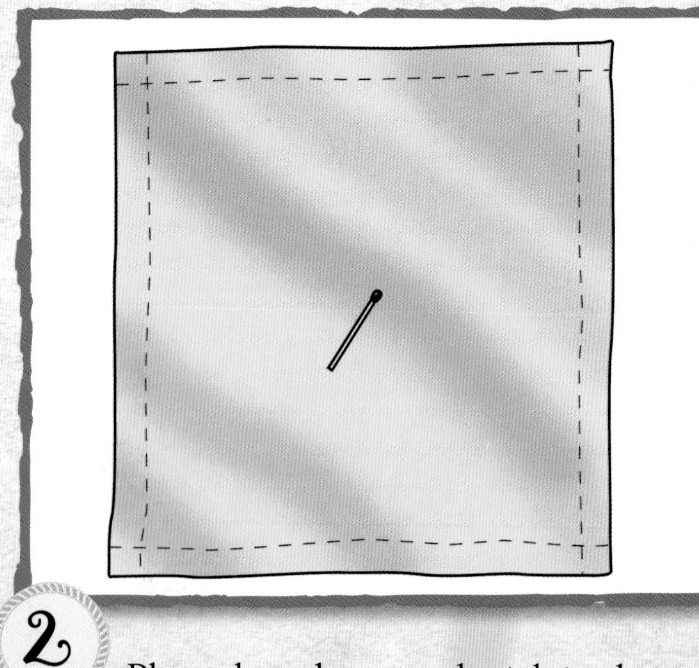

2 Place the other matchstick in the centre of the handkerchief so that your friend can see it.

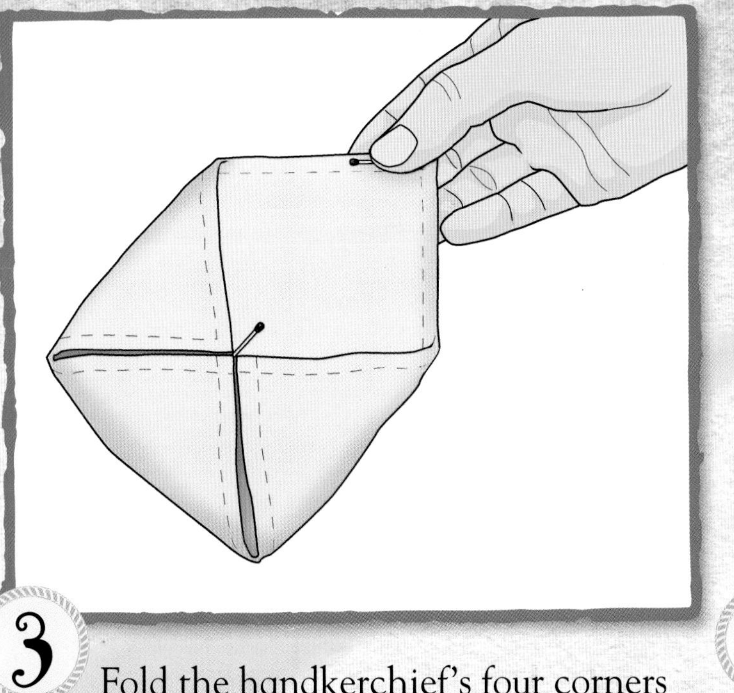

3 Fold the handkerchief's four corners to the centre, taking the corner with the hidden matchstick last. Make sure you keep hold of this corner. Pick up the folded handkerchief and turn it over.

4 Ask your friend to feel if the matchstick is still there. Guide their hand to the hidden matchstick. Then ask them to hold it through the cloth and break the matchstick into as many pieces as they want.

5 Gently shake out the handkerchief. Your friend will be amazed when the unbroken matchstick falls onto the table!

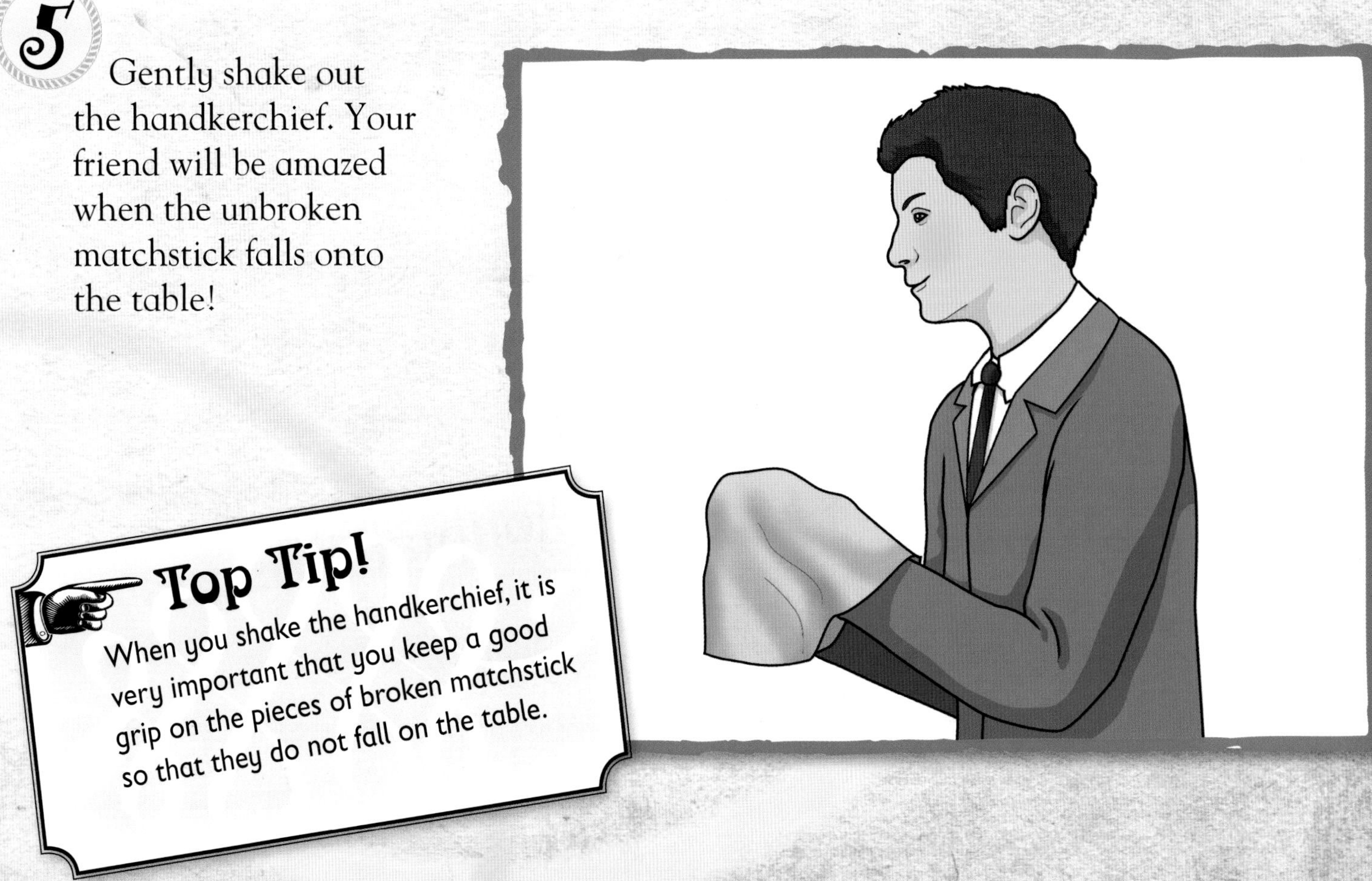

Top Tip!

When you shake the handkerchief, it is very important that you keep a good grip on the pieces of broken matchstick so that they do not fall on the table.

Pencil and paper

Balance a piece of paper on the point of a pencil and make the paper spin around and around without touching it. This looks really spooky!

Props needed...
- ✶ Sharp pencil
- ✶ Sticky putty
- ✶ Piece of paper, 6 x 15 centimetres

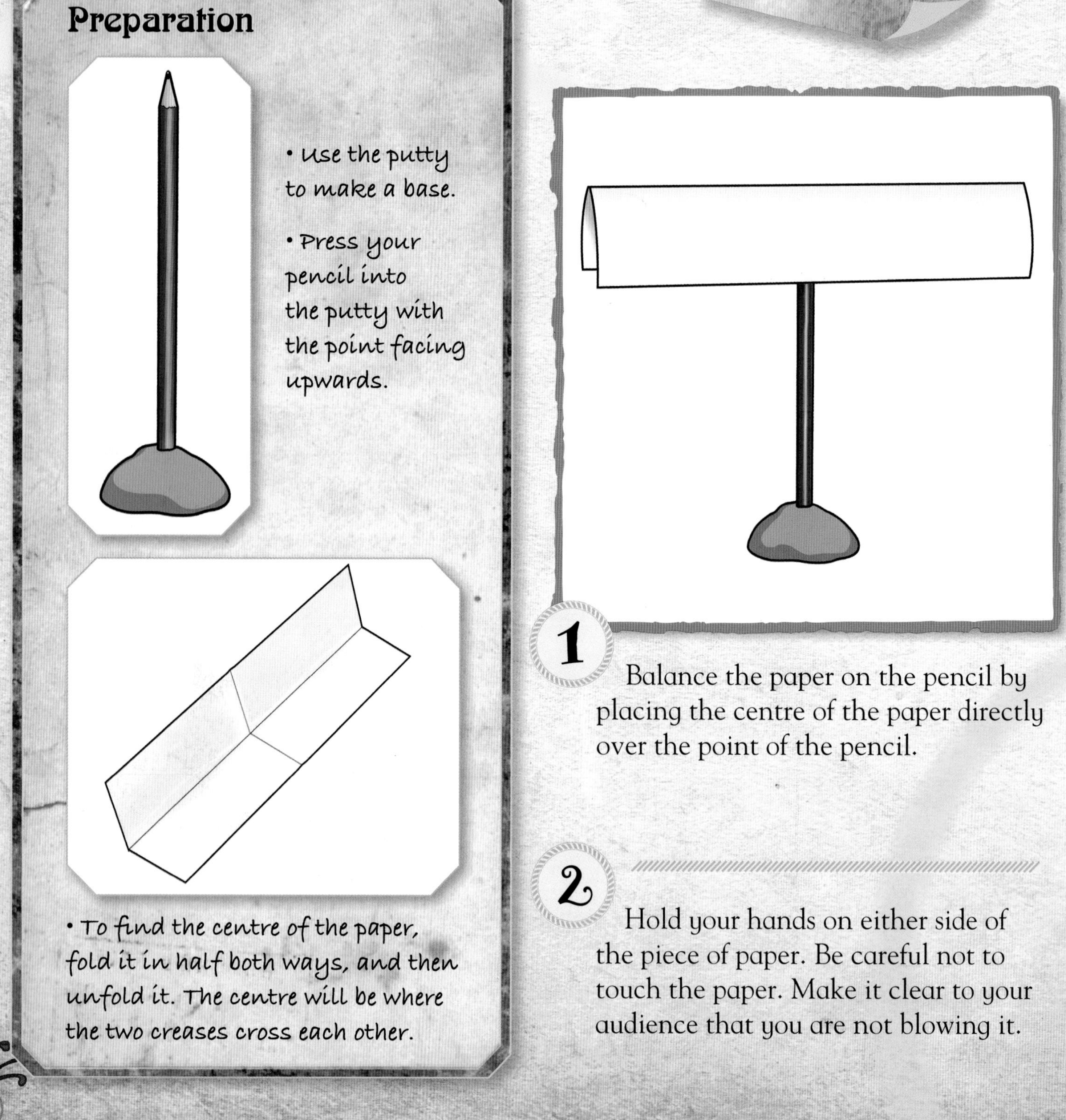

Preparation

- Use the putty to make a base.
- Press your pencil into the putty with the point facing upwards.
- To find the centre of the paper, fold it in half both ways, and then unfold it. The centre will be where the two creases cross each other.

1 Balance the paper on the pencil by placing the centre of the paper directly over the point of the pencil.

2 Hold your hands on either side of the piece of paper. Be careful not to touch the paper. Make it clear to your audience that you are not blowing it.

Top Tip!

If you can't make the paper spin around, try using a thinner piece of paper. Also, make sure the point of your pencil is really sharp.

3

Strangely enough, you will find that the paper will start to turn. With a bit of practice, you can make it change direction. See what happens when you place your hands above the paper.

4

How does it work? Well, although there may not be a draught or breeze near you, there are still air currents in any room. Your hands block these invisible currents and cause the tiny air movements that set the paper spinning.

Mysterious magician

When American William Ellsworth Robinson (1861–1918) started his career as a magician, he was known as 'Robinson, the Man of Mystery'. Later on, he changed his name to Chung Ling Soo and pretended to be Chinese. He even wore Chinese clothes on stage. Only his best friends and other magicians knew that he was not really Chinese!

◀ *To hide the fact that he was not actually Chinese, Chung Ling Soo never spoke to his audience.*

Ring of mystery

When you remove a ring that is attached to a piece of string, your friend will be left wondering how you did it – especially as they were holding both ends of the piece of string!

Props needed...
* Piece of string, 70 centimetres in length
* Handkerchief
* Borrowed ring

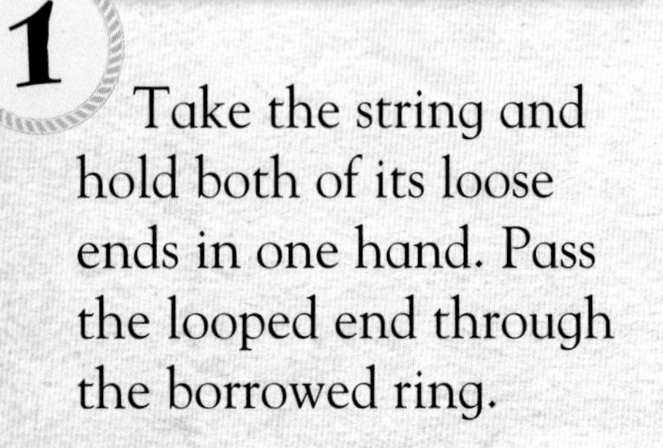

1 Take the string and hold both of its loose ends in one hand. Pass the looped end through the borrowed ring.

2 Grip the looped end of the string and carefully bring it up and over the ring.

3 The loop you make should end up at the top of the ring. The string now looks firmly tied to the ring.

Top Tip!

You can also perform this trick using a door key with a hole at one end. Use the same method as is shown for the ring.

4

Ask your friend to hold each end of the string. Tell them to hold the string loosely so that it hangs down a bit.

5

Hang the handkerchief over the ring, to hide from your friend how you do your magic.

6

As the string is loose, you will find it easy to undo the knot. Slide the top loop down and off the ring to release the ring from the string. Bring the ring out and whip the handkerchief off at the same time. Your friend is left holding both ends of the string, now with no ring!

Coining it

Everybody knows that money doesn't grow on trees. So how about conjuring a stream of coins from a plain handkerchief?

Props needed...

* 12 coins of the same value
* Handkerchief

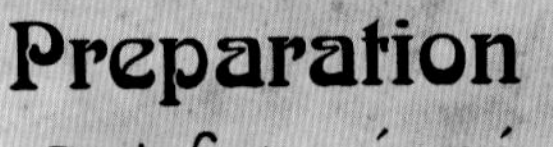

Preparation

- Put five coins in one pocket of your jacket and five more coins in another pocket.
- Hide the other two coins, one in each hand.

Top Tip!

This trick will show your ability with sleight of hand magic. In other words, doing something without your audience seeing what you are doing.

1 Let your audience look at your handkerchief so that they can be sure there is nothing hidden in it. Take it back and lay it over your left hand. Gently nudge up the hidden coin in that hand until its shape can be seen.

2 Then grip the coin through the cloth with your right thumb and first finger. Turn your right hand over so that the handkerchief now falls over your right hand and the coin can be seen.

3

Take the coin away with your left hand and make it look like you are putting the coin into your left jacket pocket. What you really do, however, is hide it in your palm when you bring your left hand out again.

4

At the same time, push up the coin that you have hidden in your right hand until its shape can be seen through the handkerchief. Grip it through the cloth with your left thumb and first finger. Then toss the handkerchief over your left hand to reveal the coin.

5

Take the coin with your right hand and pretend to put it in your right pocket. This coin is then used again – remember that you already have five coins in your pockets.

6

Repeat these moves another 10 times until it looks like you have pocketed 12 coins. Empty your pockets to prove it! Remember to add the coin in each hand to the five in each pocket at the end when you empty your pockets.

On your head

Props needed...

* Coin. The more valuable the coin is, the better

With a bit of practice, you will soon master this 'now you see it, now you don't' trick. All you need is a coin and your head!

1 Ask your friend to stand in front of you with their right hand stretched out. Show them the coin in your right hand and say, "I will count to three. When I say 'Three', I want you to grab the coin. If you get it, you can keep it."

2 Raise your right hand above your head and then bring it down again. Make sure you press the coin gently into your friend's palm when you lower it and say, "One."

Matador magic

Originally called 'The Great Soprendo', magician Geoffrey Durham used to dress as a matador for his magic shows. His catchphrase was "Piff, paff, poof." Then he changed his act. Now he often tours the United Kingdom with his one-man magic show, performing many famous illusions. These include sawing a woman in half!

▼ *Popular magician Geoffrey Durham always makes his audience laugh during his shows.*

3

Raise your hand above your head a second time and bring it down so that the coin touches your friend's palm once again. Say, "Two."

4

Repeat the move once again. But, this time, leave the coin on top of your head before you lower your hand. As you bring your hand down, say, "Three."

5

Your friend tries to snatch the coin, but finds that it's no longer there! Show them both your hands to prove that they are empty.

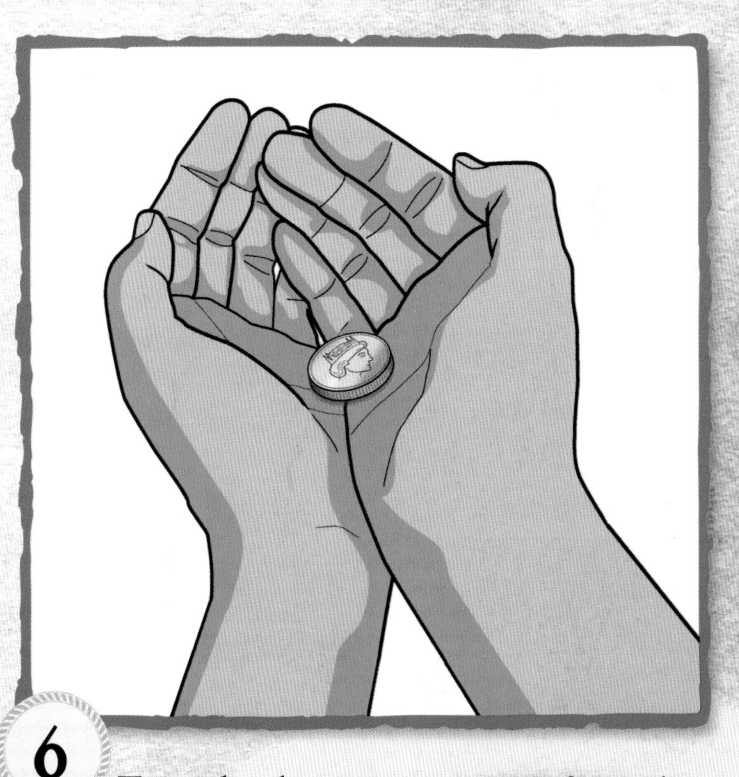

6

To make the coin reappear, first ask your friend to cup their hands and stare down at their palms. Ask them to say, "Magic money come back." Then bend over slightly so that the coin slides off your head and lands in their hands.

Breaking bread

The next time you are eating with friends and have a bread roll in your hands, why not make a coin appear out of it?

Props needed...
* Crusty bread roll
* Large coin

1 Hide the coin in the fingers of your right hand. Then pick up the bread roll with the same hand, so that the coin is hidden behind the roll.

2 Hold the bread roll up and look at it for a short while. Shake it by the side of your ear. Pretend that you can hear something. Then shake it by the ear of the person sitting next to you and say, "Can you hear anything? No?"

3 Shake the roll again beside your ear and pretend that you can still hear a noise. Then crack the bottom crust of the roll by pressing with your thumbs and pulling back the sides.

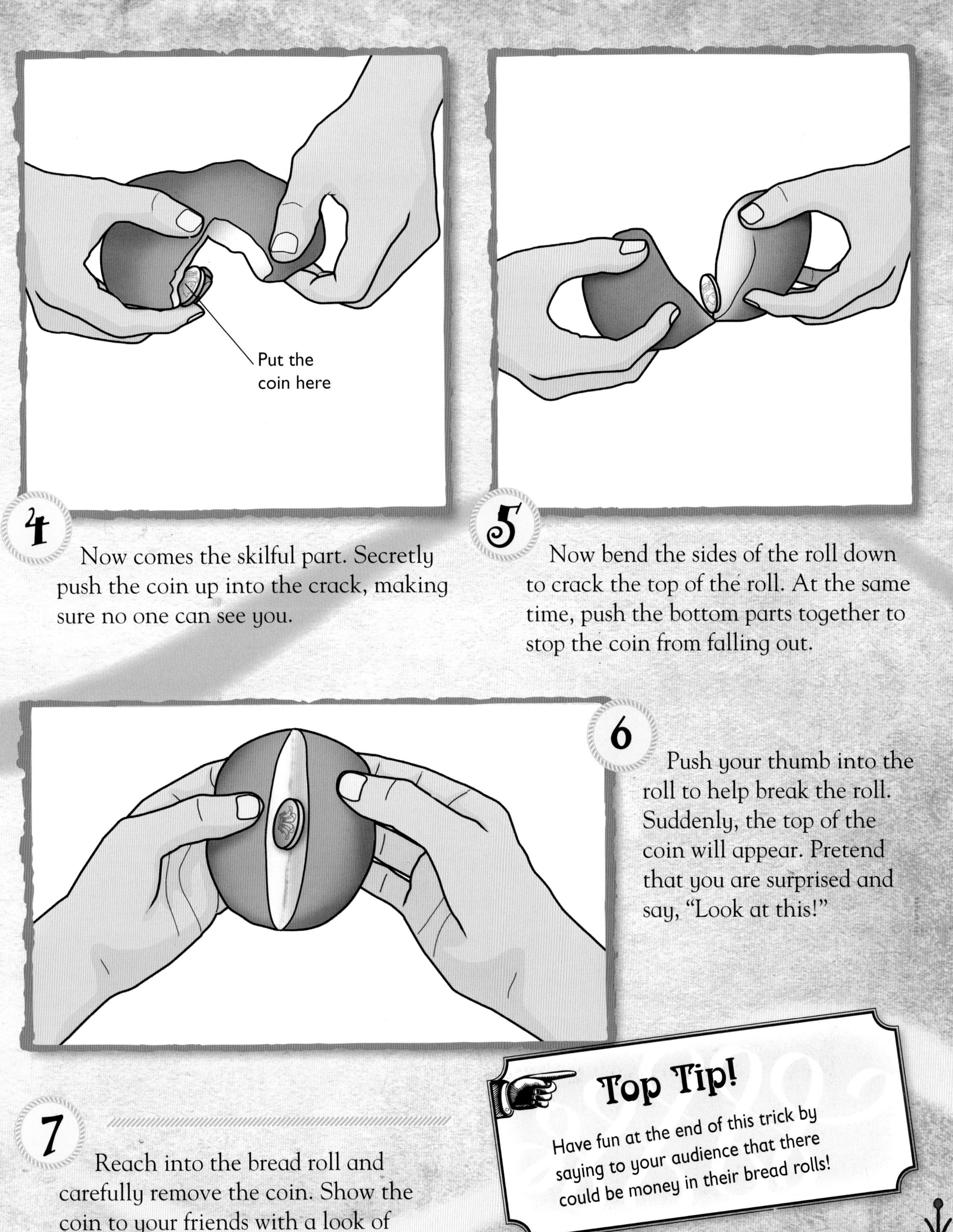

4

Now comes the skilful part. Secretly push the coin up into the crack, making sure no one can see you.

5

Now bend the sides of the roll down to crack the top of the roll. At the same time, push the bottom parts together to stop the coin from falling out.

6

Push your thumb into the roll to help break the roll. Suddenly, the top of the coin will appear. Pretend that you are surprised and say, "Look at this!"

7

Reach into the bread roll and carefully remove the coin. Show the coin to your friends with a look of amazement on your face.

Top Tip!

Have fun at the end of this trick by saying to your audience that there could be money in their bread rolls!

Up your sleeve

Now you see it, now you don't! The vanishing key trick is a real 'fooler'.

Props needed...

* Metal key with a hole in it
* Elastic cord 30 centimetres long
* Safety pin
* Magic wand

Preparation

- Attach one end of the elastic cord to the key and the other end to the safety pin.
- Fix the safety pin to the inside of your jacket's right sleeve at the top.
- Allow the key and elastic to slide down inside the sleeve. Adjust the length of the elastic so that the key hangs about 3 centimetres up from the end of the sleeve. Put the jacket on.

1

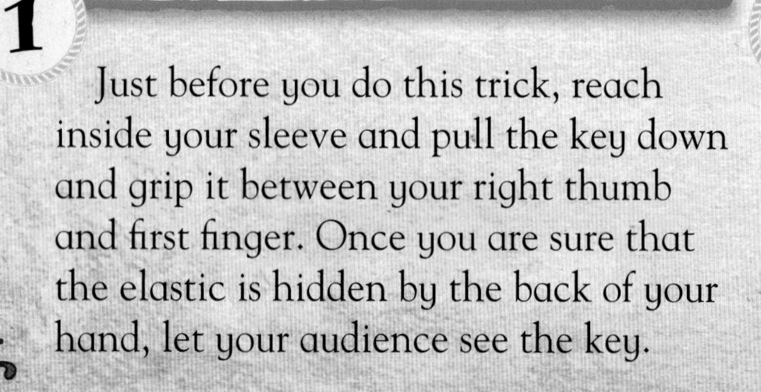

Just before you do this trick, reach inside your sleeve and pull the key down and grip it between your right thumb and first finger. Once you are sure that the elastic is hidden by the back of your hand, let your audience see the key.

2

Hold up your left-hand palm so that it is facing the audience. Let the audience see you put the key in the palm with your right hand.

3

At the same time as you close your left hand, open your right hand and let the key shoot up your sleeve. Make sure you keep your left hand closed, so that your audience thinks you are holding the key in that hand.

4

After you show the audience that your right hand is empty, pick up your magic wand with that hand. Tap your left hand three times with the wand. Then slowly open up your left hand to show that the key has really gone!

Top Tip!

Magicians call the type of prop used in this trick a 'pull'. You could make other items vanish in this way, such as a pen or a ring.

Dangerous act

The spectacular shows of magicians Siegfried and Roy featured wild animals, including the powerful white tiger. In 2003, things went badly wrong when Roy tripped as he was walking one of the tigers around the stage. The tiger tried to pick him up by biting the back of his neck. Roy was so badly hurt that the Siegfried and Roy shows had to close.

◀ Siegfried Fischbacher and Roy Horn on stage in Las Vegas with an enormous white tiger.

Tiny grooves

How do you make a matchstick jump up and down by itself? Easy. Just use the invisible grooves in your fingernails!

Props needed...
* Two matchsticks

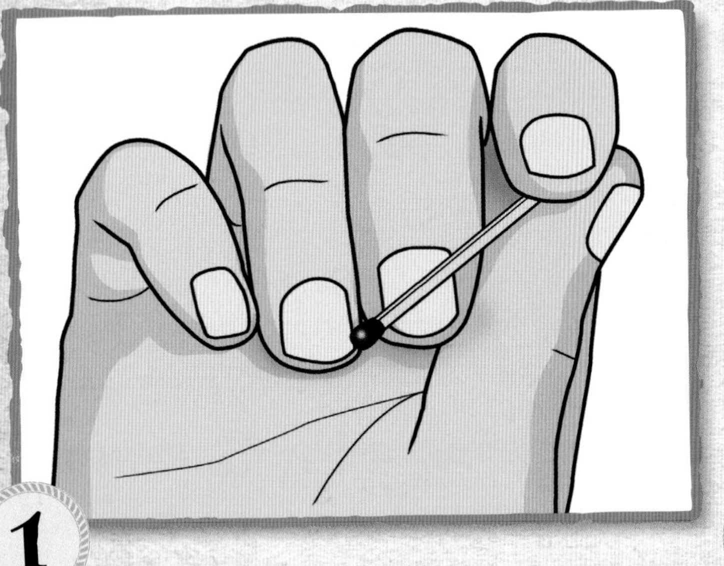

1 For this trick to work, you must hold the first matchstick in your right hand, exactly as shown. Grip the matchstick between your thumb and first finger and gently squeeze it against the nail of your second finger.

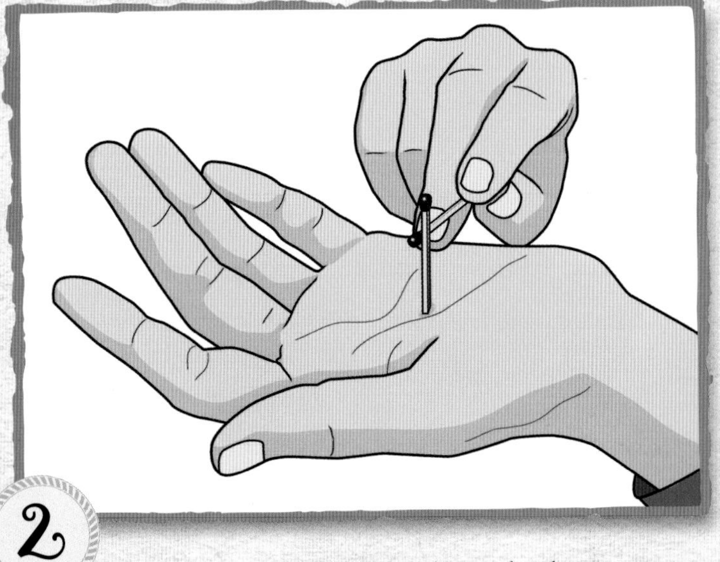

2 It is the second matchstick that jumps about. One end of this matchstick rests on the palm of your left hand. The other end sits on top of the first matchstick.

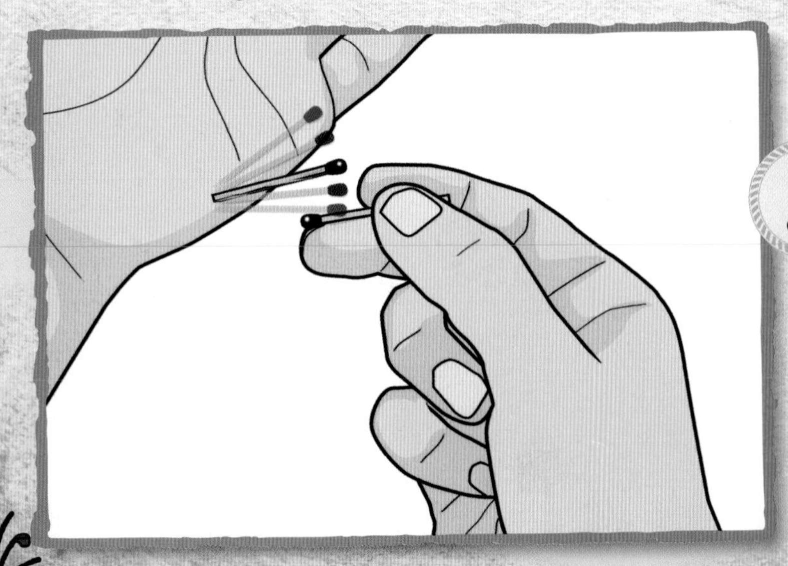

3 Squeeze the first matchstick against the nail of your second finger. This will make it skid over the tiny grooves in the nail, which causes the second matchstick to jump! If you keep pressing the first matchstick, it will skid more than 10 times before you need to adjust your grip.

MAGICAL ILLUSIONS

Simple thimble

Magicians love doing tricks with thimbles, so why not try this cheeky illusion? Using simple finger movements, you can make a thimble appear and disappear over and over again.

Props needed...
* Thimble

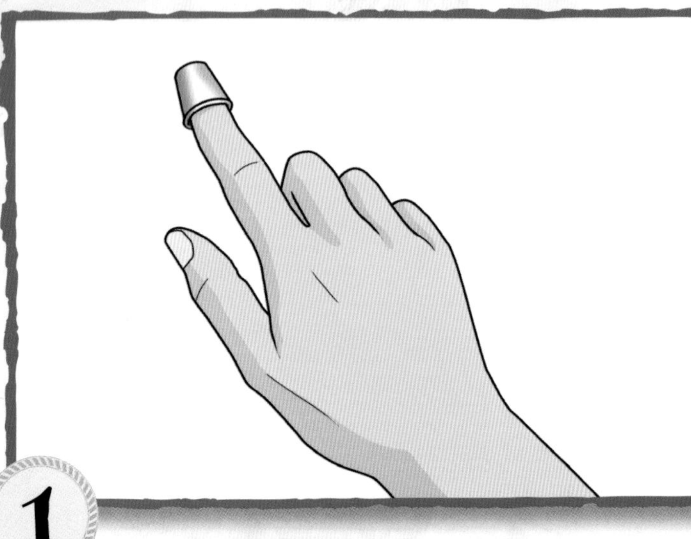

1 Fit the thimble on the first finger of your right hand.

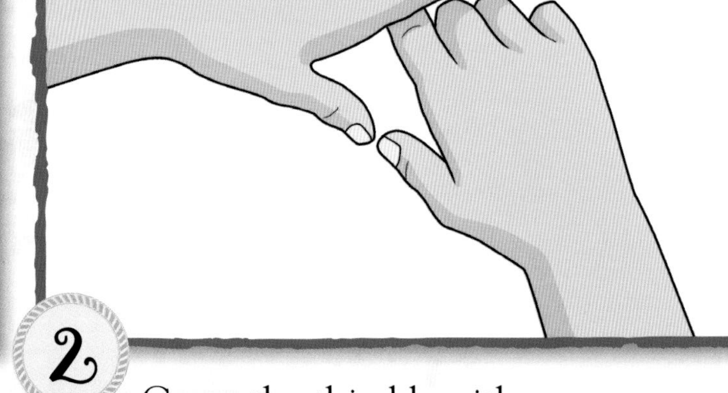

2 Cover the thimble with your open left hand so that it can't be seen.

3 When the thimble is hidden, close your right hand. Keep your right hand hidden under your left hand.

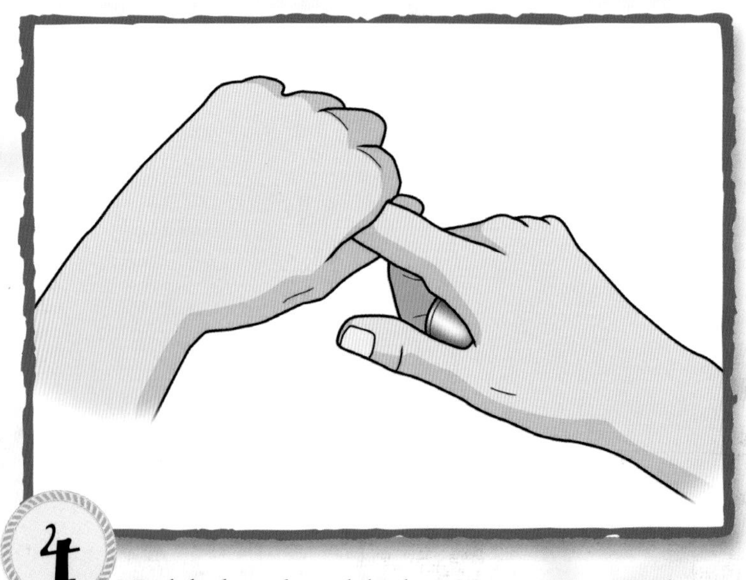

4 Hold the thimble between your right hand's second finger and thumb. As soon as you have done this, shoot your first finger forward and grip it with the fingers of your left hand.

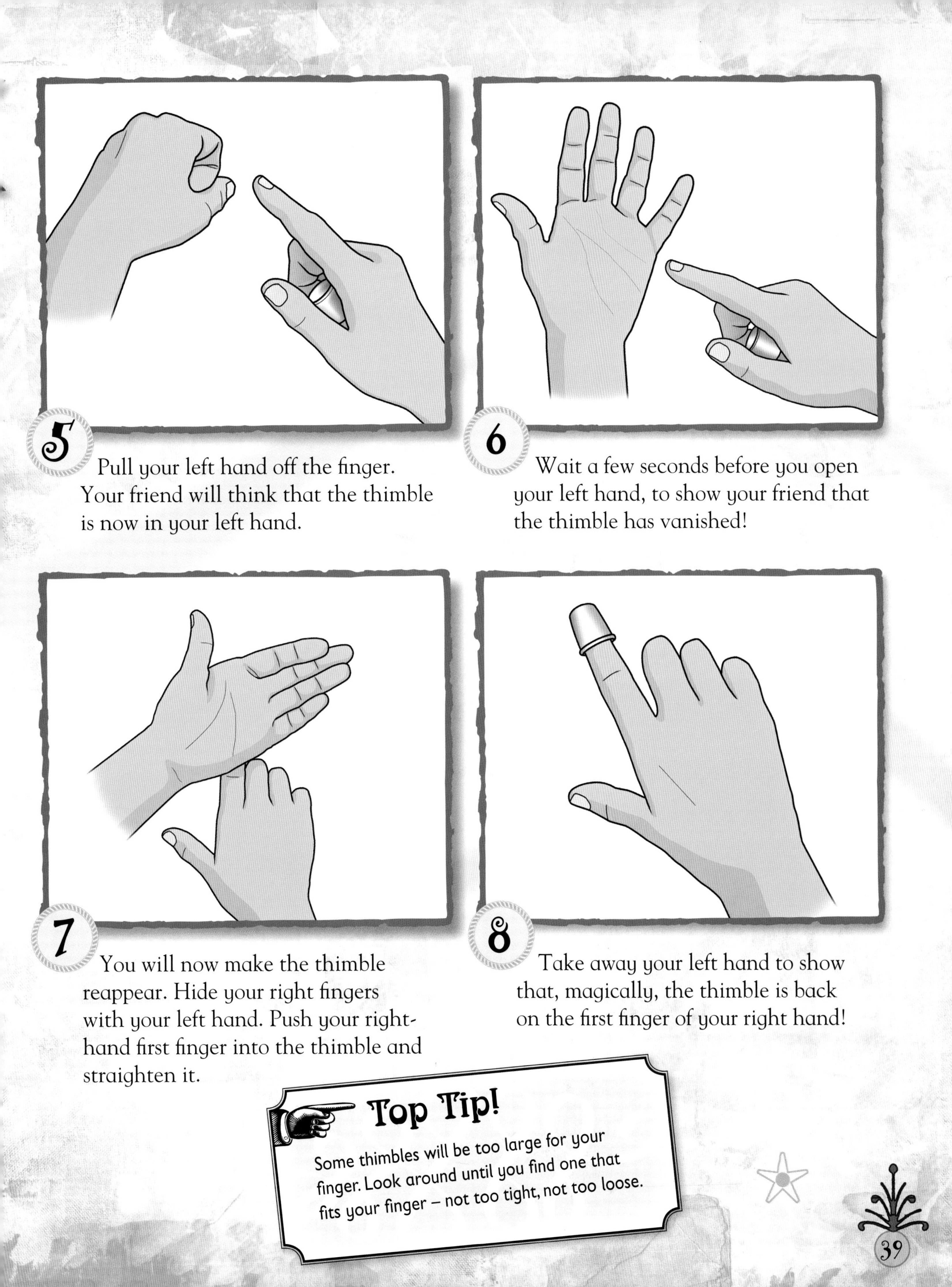

5 Pull your left hand off the finger. Your friend will think that the thimble is now in your left hand.

6 Wait a few seconds before you open your left hand, to show your friend that the thimble has vanished!

7 You will now make the thimble reappear. Hide your right fingers with your left hand. Push your right-hand first finger into the thimble and straighten it.

8 Take away your left hand to show that, magically, the thimble is back on the first finger of your right hand!

Top Tip!

Some thimbles will be too large for your finger. Look around until you find one that fits your finger – not too tight, not too loose.

Sense of direction

This is an effective illusion that you can perform at any time. The only thing you will need is a clever miniature traffic sign, which you can keep in your pocket.

Props needed...
* Small piece of white card
* Scissors
* Glue
* Pencil

Preparation

• Draw or photocopy the street sign onto the white card. Then draw the arrows as shown. Fold the traffic sign in half along the dotted line and glue the two halves together.

• There are many ways of holding the street sign. If you hold the sign in position A in your left hand, the arrows on both sides will be pointing the same way when you turn the sign with your right-hand thumb.

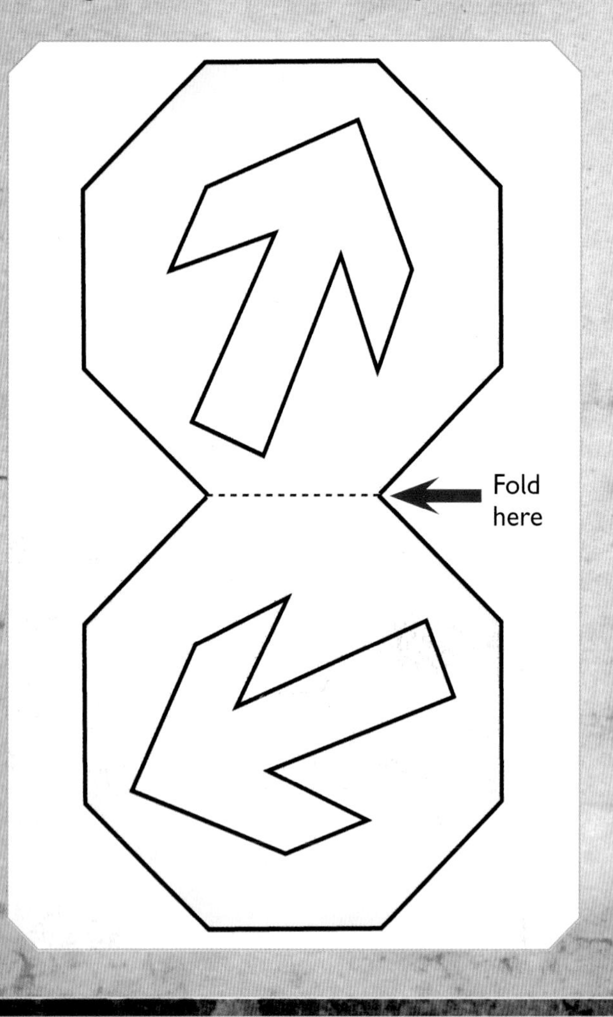

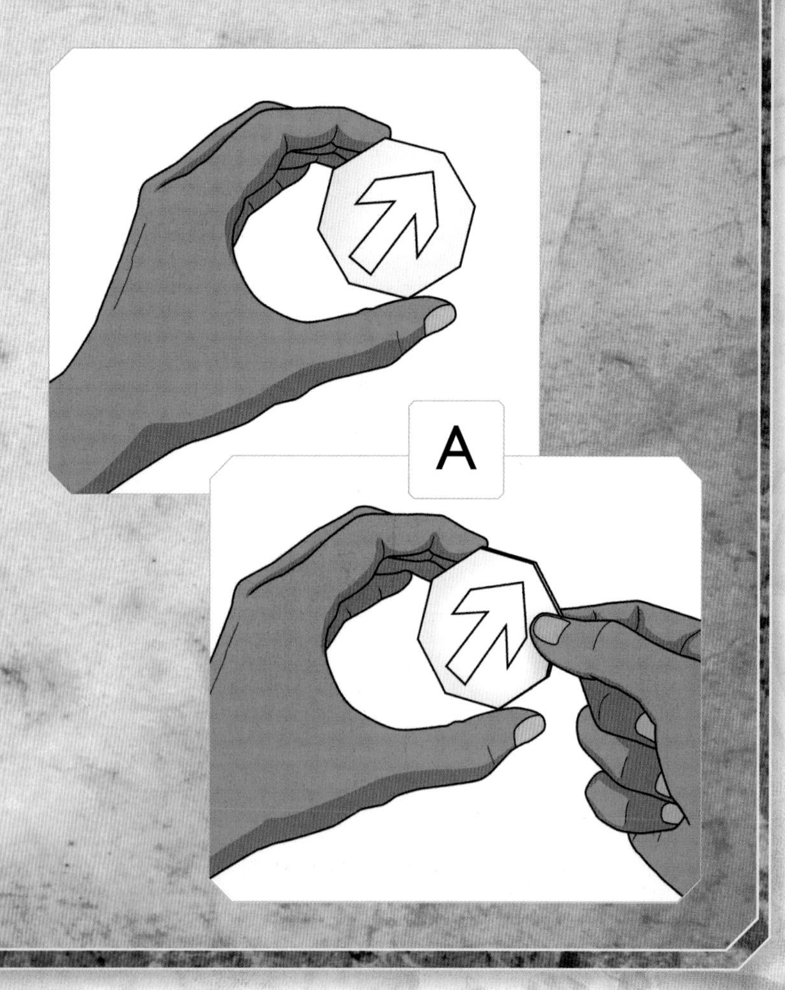

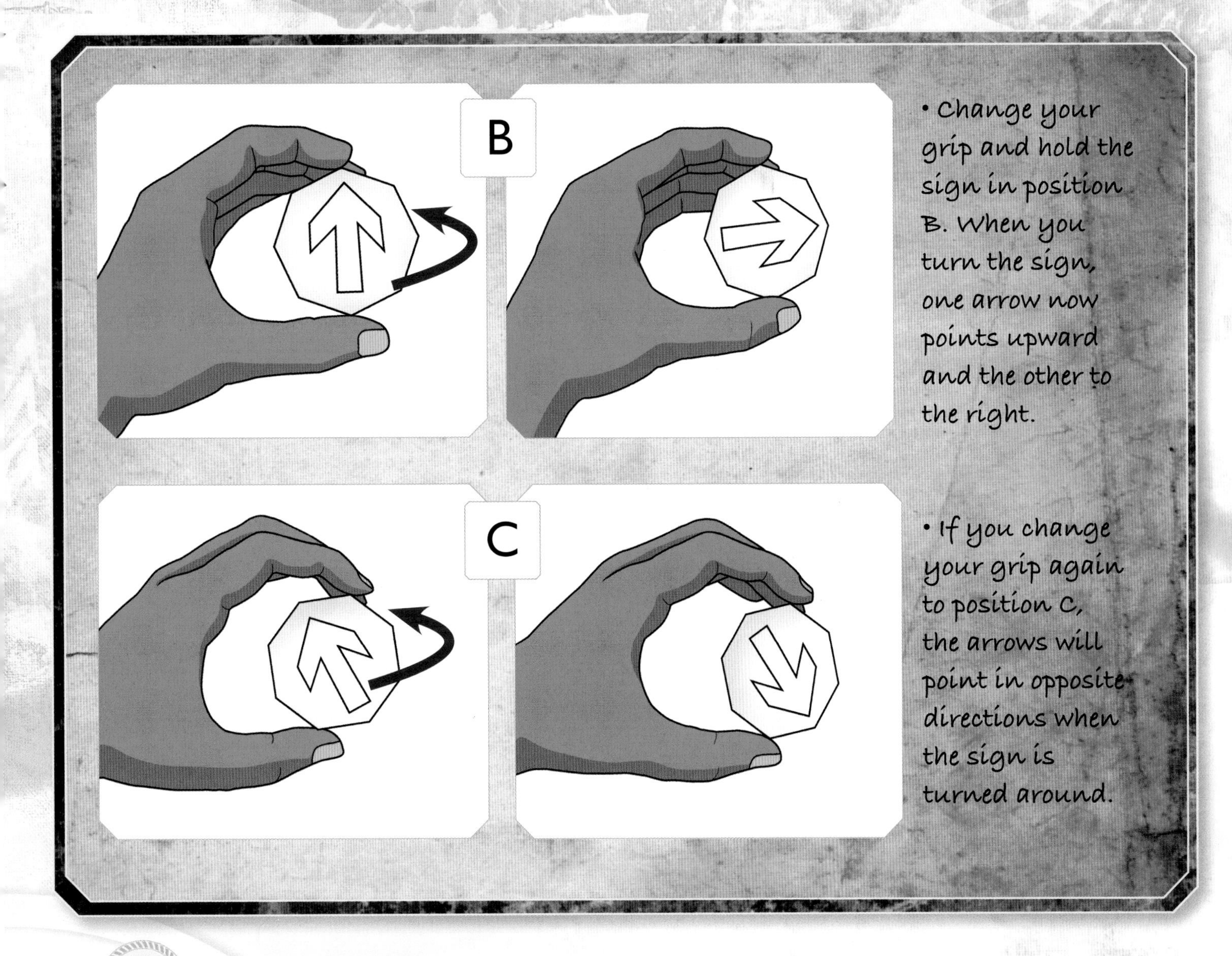

1 Tell a story, such as this one, while you hold up and turn the traffic sign.

"I went for a drive with my father. He was the driver and I was the navigator. I told him to drive straight ahead (A), and for a while everything went fine. I wanted him to keep straight ahead (B) but he decided he wanted to go to the right.

By the time I had convinced him to go straight ahead again, I found that we had been driving around in circles (C) and finally ended up where we started.

Why don't parents ever do what they're told?"

Top Tip!

Make up a story to suit yourself. Keep things simple for the best effect. Put the traffic sign in your pocket when you have finished.

Upside-down card

How do you find the one card that your friend chose from a pack of playing cards? It's not difficult – all you do is secretly turn the card at the bottom of the pack upside down!

Props needed...

* Pack of playing cards

Preparation

• Before you start the trick, turn over the bottom card in the pack.

1 Spread the cards and ask your friend to take one – they must not show it to you. Keep the bottom card hidden. Once your friend has a card, tidy the pack and hold it in one hand.

Ask your friend to look at the front of the card and remember it. While they are doing this, secretly turn the pack over so that the bottom, upside-down card is now at the top. The rest of the pack is face up underneath this card.

2

Ask your friend to put their card back somewhere in the middle of the pack. They will not notice that the pack, apart from the top card, is upside down. Then say, "I am going to put the pack behind my back to try and find your card without looking at the cards."

3

As soon as the cards are out of sight behind your back, turn the top card the other way so that now the only upside-down card in the pack will be your friend's card. This is somewhere in the middle of the pack.

4

Bring the pack out and spread the cards across the table face up. There will be one face-down card in the middle of the cards. Ask your friend to say the name of their card. Then ask them to turn over the face-down card. This will be their card!

Clowning around

Hans Moretti's box illusion is truly amazing! The magician is first tied in chains and sealed into a box. Twelve people from the audience are asked to push long swords into the box from all sides. Is Moretti injured? No! When he comes out of the box, not only is he unharmed; he is dressed as a clown, complete with clown makeup, and is holding two doves.

◀ *How does Hans Moretti survive all these swords? It's a complete mystery!*

Safety first

Link two ordinary safety pins together and close them up securely. Then, in a flash, pull them apart. Amazingly, they will magically separate while still closed.

Props needed...

* Two large safety pins

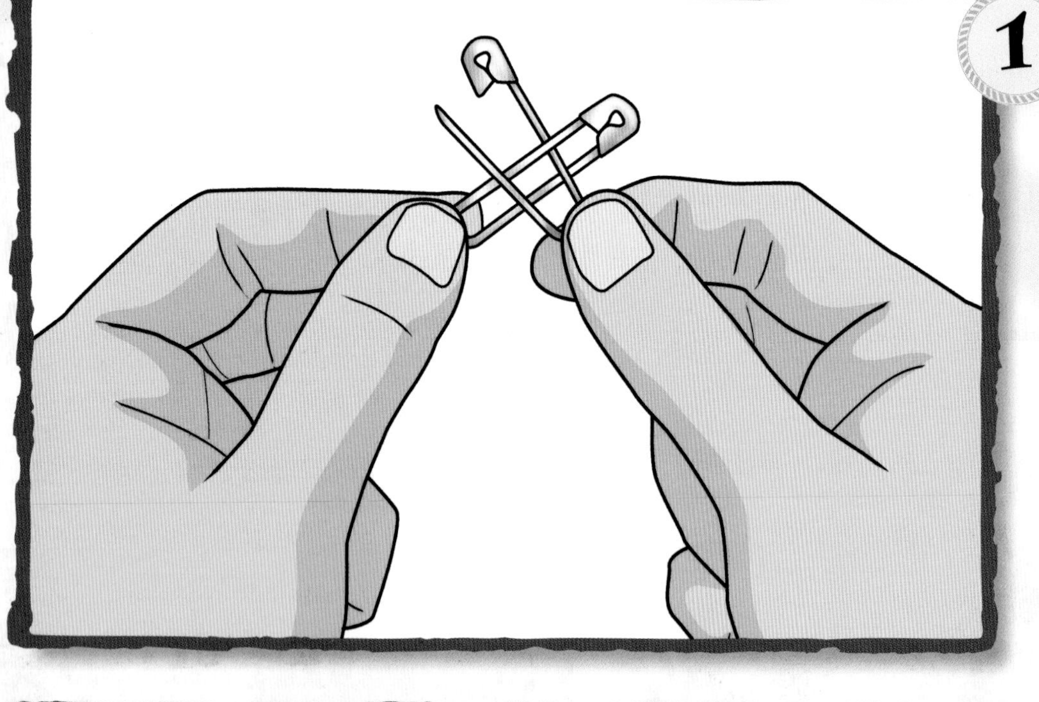

1

Link the two safety pins together by putting one open safety pin through a closed safety pin. Close the open safety pin. Then hold the two linked safety pins by their ends.

2

Make sure that the opening and non-opening bars of each pin are in the position shown in this illustration.

3 Once sure that you are holding the safety pins correctly, grip them tightly. Now pull sharply in opposite directions.

4 The safety pins separate, but stay closed! In fact, they open and close so quickly that you can't see it happen. Ask someone in the audience to look at the safety pins to make sure that there was nothing wrong with them.

▲ *Many magicians now perform the amazing Zigzag Girl trick.*

Zigzag Girl

Robert Harbin's (1909–1978) Zigzag Girl is a scary illusion. After a girl steps into a cabinet, two big blades are pushed through the cabinet, slicing the cabinet, and maybe the girl, into three pieces. When the centre section is pushed to one side, a small door is opened to show the girl's stomach. Her head and her right foot can be seen in the top and bottom sections. When the centre section is put back, the girl walks out of the cabinet unharmed!

One-way street

There are 19 cards in a pack that have a 'one-way' design. These cards can be easily spotted when turned around. You can use these cards for many illusions, including this neat trick.

Props needed...

* Pack of playing cards

Preparation

• Lay out the 19 playing cards below, making sure that they are the same way up as shown. These cards look different when turned.
• Gather up the 19 cards so that they stay the same way up. Place this stack face down on a table.
• Put the Joker on top of this stack, and the other cards on the Joker.

1 Tell your friend that you will not be needing all the cards from the pack. Spread out the entire pack face up and take the 19 cards that you have secretly chosen. This is easy to do – you just have to look through the pack until you see the Joker. Put the Joker and all the cards underneath it to one side.

2

After you have let your friend shuffle the 19 cards, take them back. Then spread them out, face down, in your hands. Ask your friend to take a card, to look at it, and remember it.

3

While your friend is looking at their card, secretly turn around the cards you are holding. Then ask your friend to put back their card in the pack you are holding. Also ask them to shuffle the cards again so that you cannot possibly know where it is in the pack.

4

Take the cards back and spread them face up in a line across the table. Look for the one that is a different way up to the rest. That one is your friend's card.

5

Ask your friend to hold your wrist as you pass your hand over the line of cards. Pretend that you are using special magical powers to find the correct card. After about 10 seconds, pick up the card your friend chose and give it to them.

Top Tip!

Some packs of cards have one-way designs on their back, such as an animal picture. Look out for packs such as these, so that you can do the trick with the complete pack of 52 cards.

Crazy shoelaces

You will not believe that this trick really works until you try it for yourself. All you need are two coloured shoelaces and a magic wand. The rest is just pure magic.

Props needed...
* Red shoelace and yellow shoelace
* Magic wand

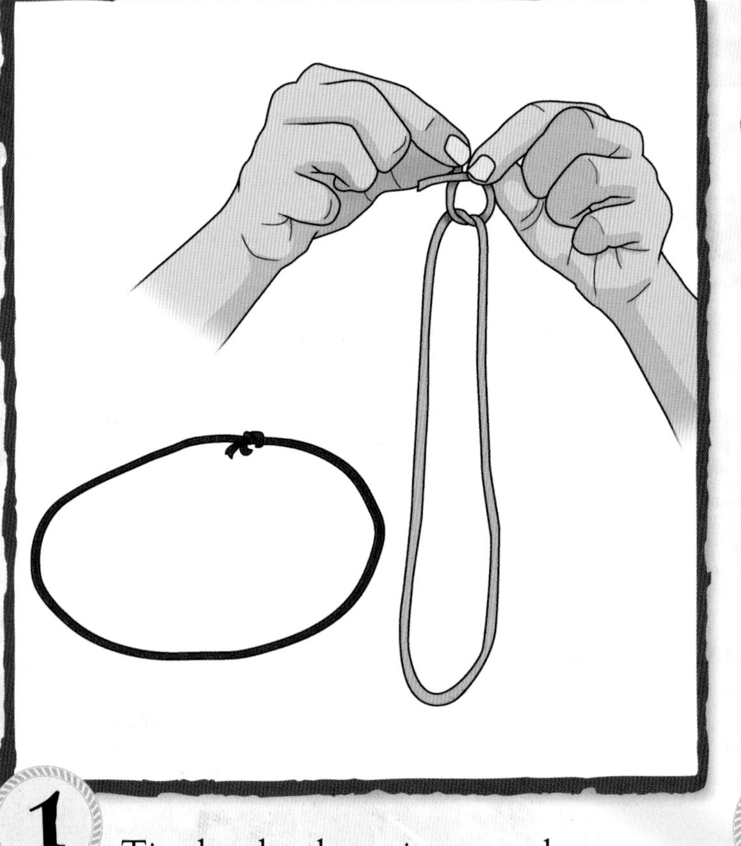

1 Tie the shoelaces into two loops.

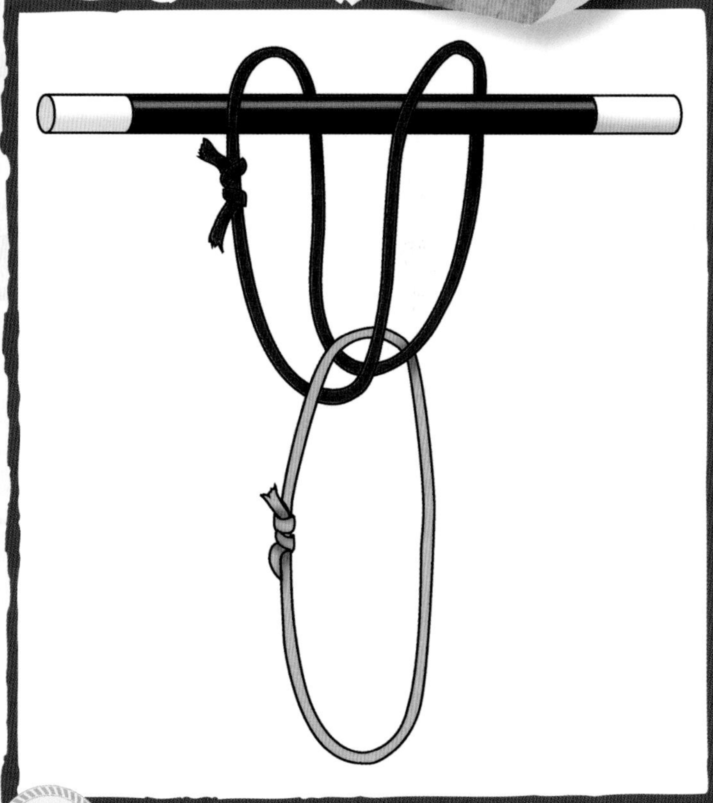

2 Thread the red loop through the other loop. Then slip the red shoelace onto the magic wand.

Top Tip!

Coloured shoelaces are sometimes not very easy to find. Fortunately, coloured string or coloured ribbons will work just as well!

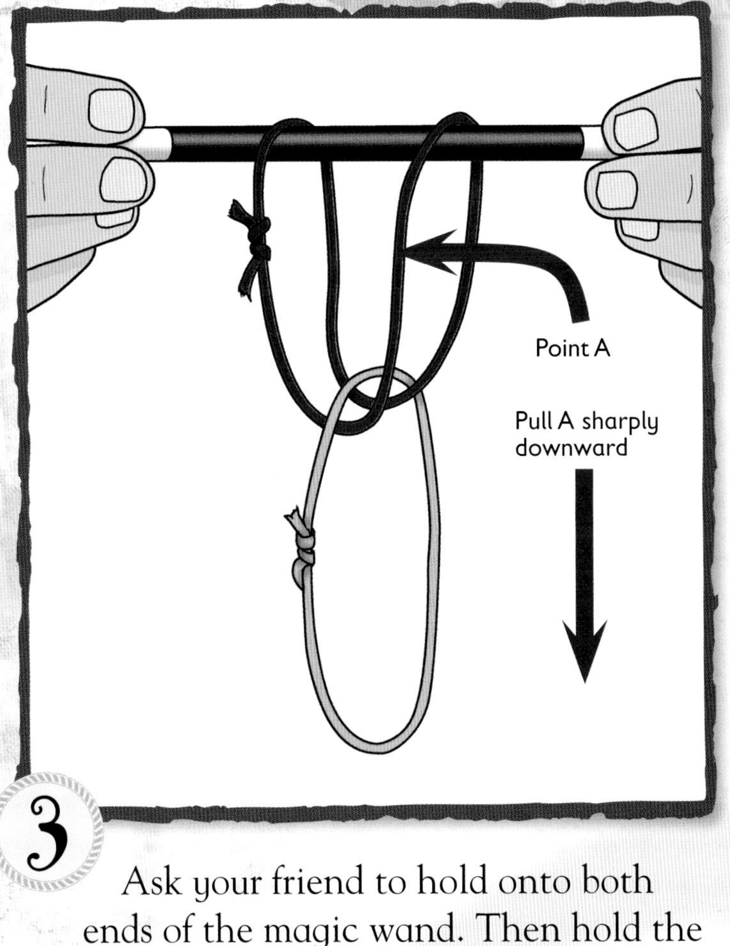

3

Ask your friend to hold onto both ends of the magic wand. Then hold the red loop at point A. Pull downwards very sharply and you will find that the two laces instantly change places.

4

The yellow shoelace is now threaded onto the wand and the red shoelace now hangs down loose.

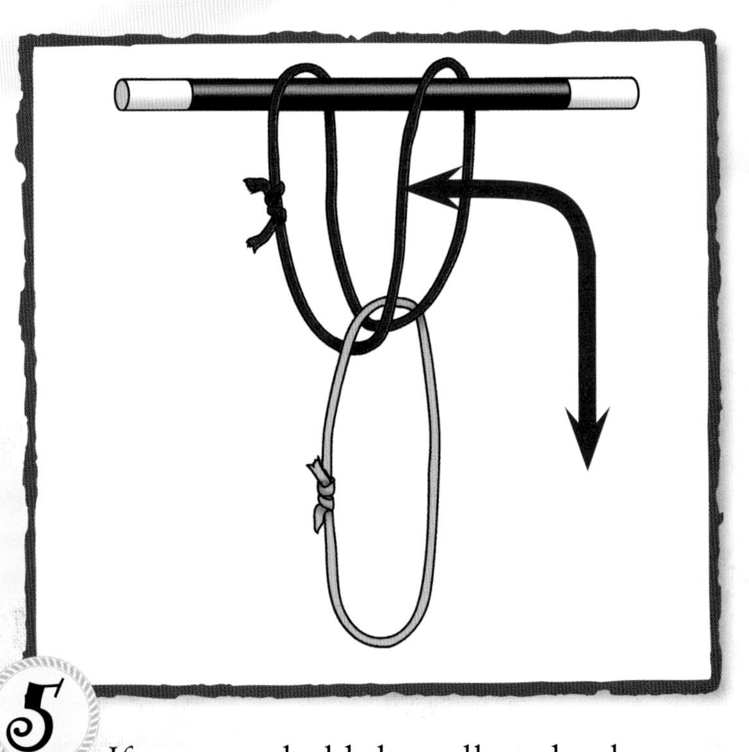

5

If you now hold the yellow shoelace at the same place that you held the red shoelace and pull, the two shoelaces will change places again!

Vanishing cards

Magician Paul Potassy's best trick involves two seated spectators, who deal themselves 20 playing cards each and sit on them. Potassy then magically moves one person's 20 cards to the other person so that one person now sits on 40 cards. The cards under the other person vanish! Neither spectator has any idea how he does it.

▶ *Paul Potassy's amazing card trick always delights his audiences.*

Jumpin' Joker

It must be magic when a card that your friend is holding in their hand suddenly vanishes and then reappears in your pocket!

Props needed...

* Pack of playing cards
* Handkerchief
* Scissors

Preparation

• Remove the two Jokers, the King of Hearts and the King of Clubs from your pack of playing cards. Put the rest of the pack aside.

• Cut out a piece from the end of one of the Jokers. This should be 20 x 25 millimetres.

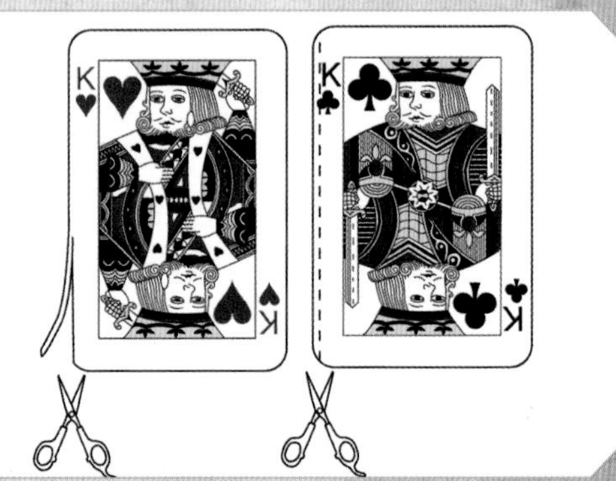

• Remove the two Kings and cut off a thin strip 1.5 millimetres wide from their long, left edge. This makes them slightly narrower.

• Put the Joker you have not cut in your pocket.

1 To do this trick, sit at a table with your friend sitting opposite you.

2 Hold the three cards in your left hand and show them to your friend. The cut part of the Joker is hidden behind the top King of Hearts.

3

Carefully close the cards up and give them to your friend to hold. Make sure that the cut end is between their thumb and first finger.

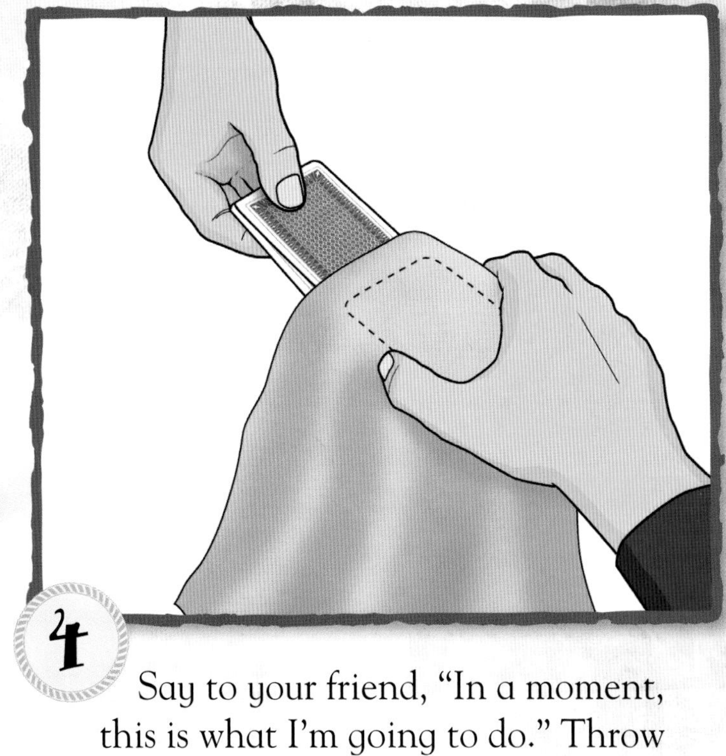

4

Say to your friend, "In a moment, this is what I'm going to do." Throw the handkerchief over the cards and your friend's hand. Then grip the edges of the cards and pull the handkerchief away. This will take the Joker away in the handkerchief, as it is wider than the other two cards. Your friend will not feel anything! Drop the handkerchief with the hidden Joker into your lap.

5

Now say, "Hold onto the cards. I'm going to cover your hand with the handkerchief again and make the Joker jump into my pocket." Pretend that you are magically taking the Joker away from your friend and throwing it into your pocket. Remove the handkerchief and leave it on the table. Ask your friend to look for the Joker. It has gone!

6

Remove the other Joker from your pocket. Your friend will believe that it jumped into your pocket, as you said it would!

Top Tip!

You don't have to hurry to hide the Joker in your lap. Your friend will lift the handkerchief when looking for the Joker. That's the time to slip the Joker secretly into your pocket.

Last straw

Thread a piece of string through a drinking straw and cut both of them in half. Then, magically, restore the piece of string to its original length. You will have to practise this daring trick a few times before you try it on a friend.

Props needed...

* Straw
* String, 1 metre long
* Scissors
* Hobby knife

Preparation

• Ask an adult to cut an 8-centimetre slit along the centre of the straw.

Cut slit here

1 Pick up the straw with the slit side hidden from your friend. Thread the string through the straw.

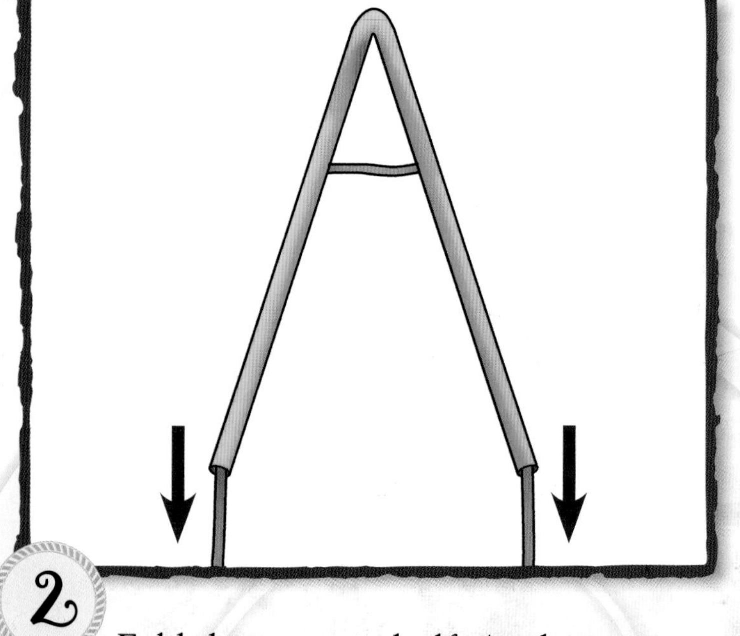

2 Fold the straw in half. At the same time, pull down the two ends of the string. This will make part of the string come through the slit in the straw.

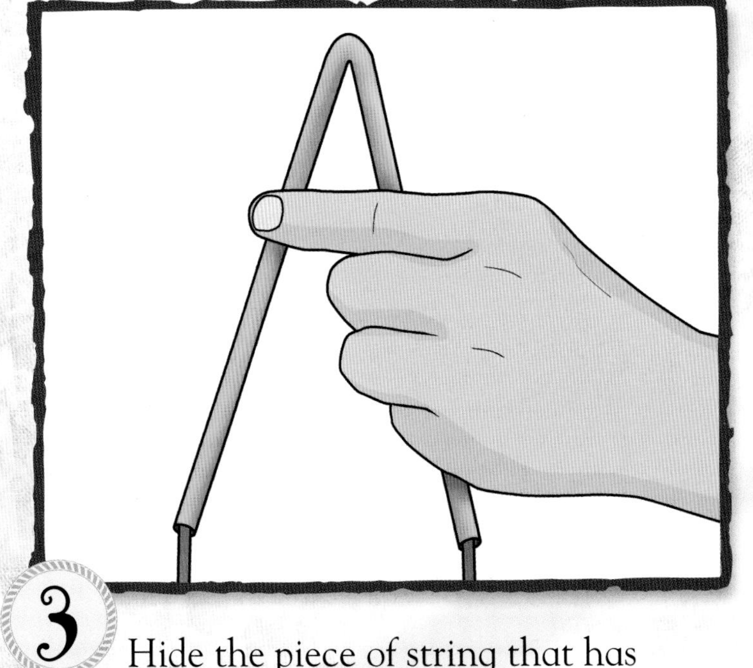

3 Hide the piece of string that has come through the straw with your left first finger and thumb.

4 Cut through the centre of the straw with the scissors. Your friend will think that you are also cutting the string!

5 Hold up the two halves of the straw in your left hand. With your finger and thumb, you must hide the section of string that you pulled through the slit.

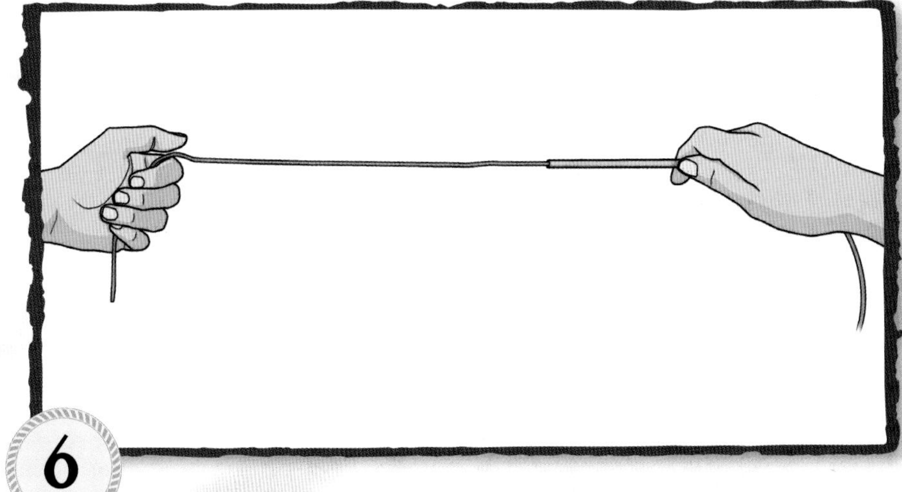

6 Hold the two cut ends of the straw together and slowly pull out the string. Amazingly, it will be one complete length of string again!

Top Tip!

Keep your secret safe: quietly put the two halves of the straw in your pocket before your friend has a chance to discover how you did this impressive trick.

Bangle wangle

This trick may have been invented by Harry Houdini, perhaps the most famous magician of all time. Here, you magically remove a bangle dangling from a piece of string tied to your wrists, without undoing the knots!

Props needed...

* Two identical bangles
* Piece of string, 1.5 metres long
* Jacket with an inside pocket

Preparation

• Slip one of the bangles over your right hand and gently push it up your sleeve until it is out of sight. Keep this bangle hidden.

Hidden bangle

• Put the string and the other bangle on the table.

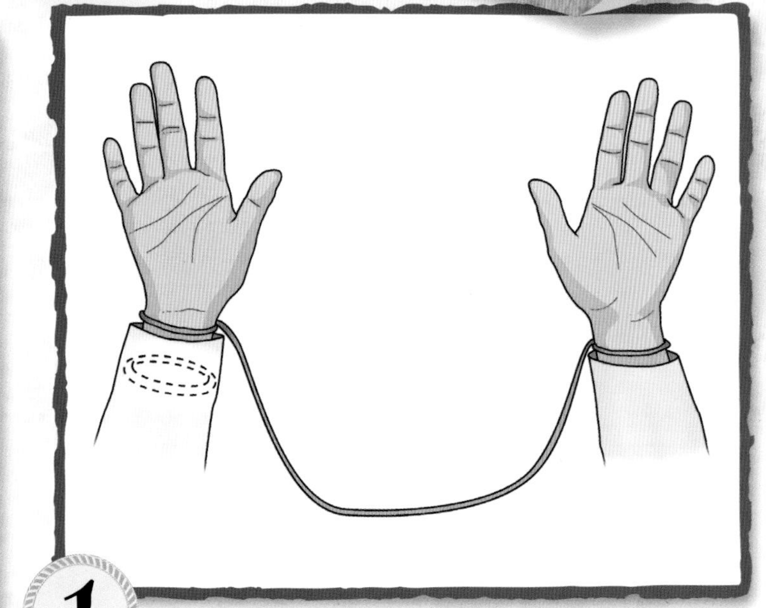

1 Ask your friend to tie the string around each of your wrists. They should leave about 40 centimetres of string between each wrist. Ask them to check that the string will not come undone and that the bangle is not broken.

Top Tip!

Practise this trick until you can do it smoothly and really quickly. The trick looks even better if you use soft white rope or a length of wide ribbon.

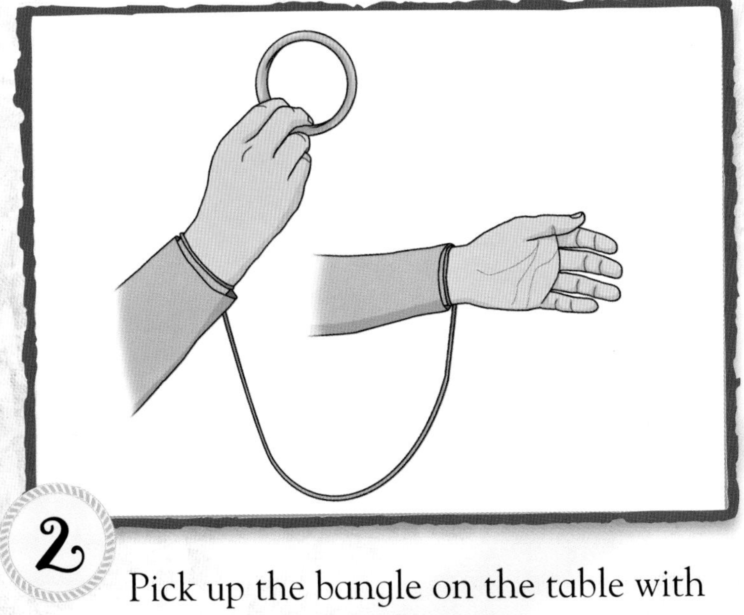

2

Pick up the bangle on the table with your right hand.

3

Say "Watch!" and quickly turn your back on your friend. Put the bangle in your inside jacket pocket. Pull the hidden bangle from your sleeve, pass it over your hand and onto the string. Leave it dangling on the string.

4

Turn around to face your friend. Ask them to examine the knots again, to make sure that you have not secretly loosened the knots to slip the bangle onto the string.

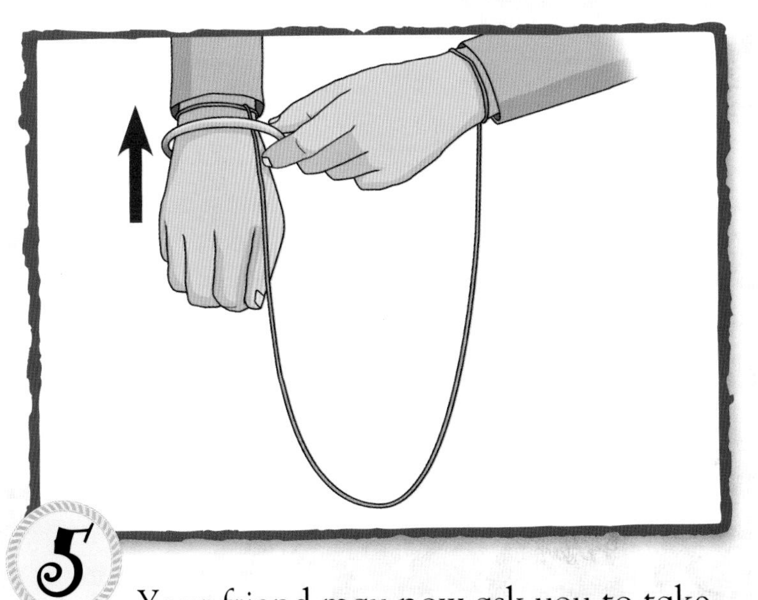

5

Your friend may now ask you to take the bangle off the string. To do this, turn your back again. Then slide the bangle off the string, over your hand and wrist, and hide it up your right sleeve. Reach into your inside jacket pocket with your left hand and remove the other bangle. Turn around and show your friend the loose bangle!

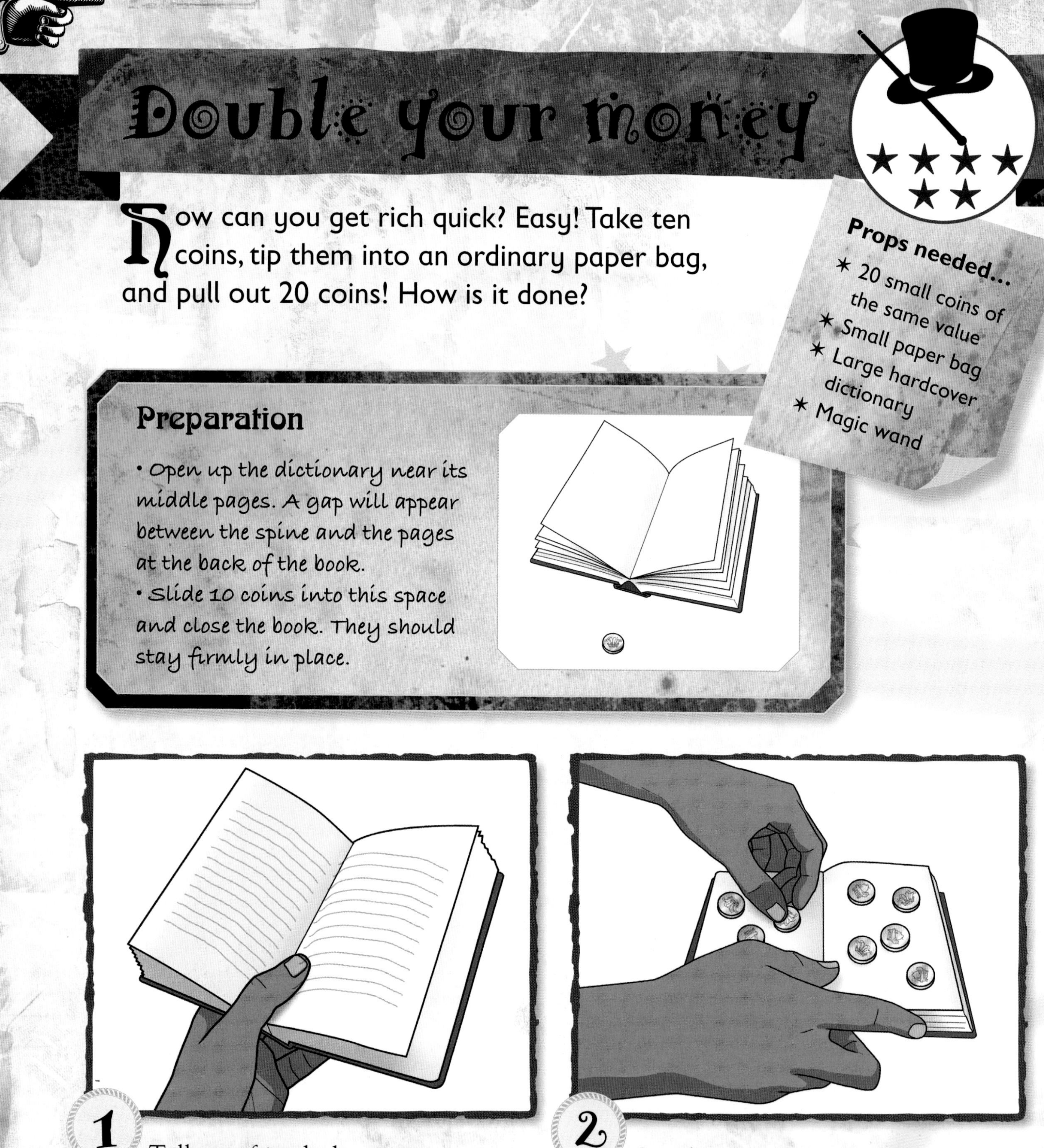

Double your money

How can you get rich quick? Easy! Take ten coins, tip them into an ordinary paper bag, and pull out 20 coins! How is it done?

Props needed...
* 20 small coins of the same value
* Small paper bag
* Large hardcover dictionary
* Magic wand

Preparation

• Open up the dictionary near its middle pages. A gap will appear between the spine and the pages at the back of the book.
• Slide 10 coins into this space and close the book. They should stay firmly in place.

1 Tell your friends that you are going to look up the word 'magic'. Pick up the dictionary and open it near the middle. Look for the word 'magic' and read the definition to your friends.

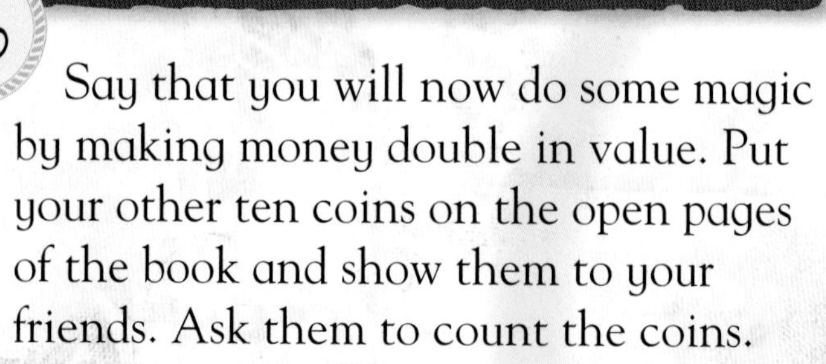

2 Say that you will now do some magic by making money double in value. Put your other ten coins on the open pages of the book and show them to your friends. Ask them to count the coins.

Top Tip!

Practise this illusion a few times before your performance. Most dictionaries can be heavy and difficult to hold if you are not used to it.

3 Ask your friends to look inside the paper bag to make sure that it is empty. Then tip all the coins into the open bag. The ten coins hidden inside the dictionary's spine will also drop into the bag. Your friends won't see this happen!

4 Put the book down and scrunch up the neck of the bag. Pick up your magic wand and say, "Hubble bubble, make my money double." Ask a friend to open the bag and count the coins. Your friends saw you put ten coins in the bag; now there are 20!

Linking rings

Magician Michael Vincent performs the beautiful Chinese linking rings trick. First, he allows the audience to inspect closely eight large, solid-steel rings. Then, he magically passes solid metal through solid metal, linking and unlinking the rings. He joins them in pairs, threes and even into a long chain. Finally, he unlinks the rings and hands them out to the audience again.

▼ *Michael Vincent is also a master of magic illusions using playing cards.*

Mind reading

Your friend uses playing cards to choose a word in a book. They do not tell you what the word is. You then use your magical skills to read their mind and write down the correct word!

Props needed...

* Reading book with more than 64 pages
* Pack of playing cards
* Paper
* Pencil

Preparation

• Arrange the pack so that the following cards are on top of the pack – a six, a four, a five and a seven. Their suit does not matter.

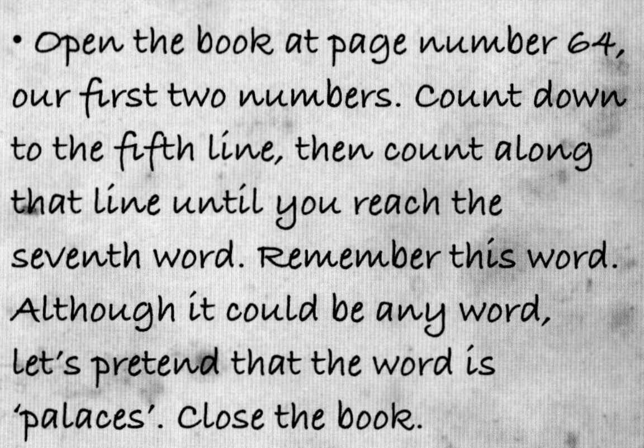

• Open the book at page number 64, our first two numbers. Count down to the fifth line, then count along that line until you reach the seventh word. Remember this word. Although it could be any word, let's pretend that the word is 'palaces'. Close the book.

Top Tip!

Looking at the book distracts your friend's attention from what actually happened with the cards. They will have no idea that the cards that they use are the original top four cards!

1 Ask your friend to lift off about half of the pack and put the cards to one side. As you say, "We'll mark where you cut like this", lift up the remainder of the pack and place it across your friend's cards. Then hand the book to your friend and ask them to make sure that the book is real and that all the pages are different.

2

Lift off the top half of the pack and place it to one side. Point to the lower half and say, “You could have cut the pack anywhere. Please take the first two cards. They’re going to represent a page number in the book.” Then ask them, “What are they? Oh! A six and a four. Please turn to page 64 in the book.” They then find the page.

3

Then say, “Take the next card. Don’t tell me what it is. Its number will be the line on the page. So count down to the line number.” They find the line.

4

Say, “Take the next card. This will show the word that I want you to think about. Count along the line until you get to the word. Don’t say it out loud – just think of it.” Now use your acting skills and pretend to think for about 10 seconds. Then write down the word that you have memorized – palaces – and show it to your amazed friend!

Blown away

Tony Slydini’s (1900–1991) best trick was that of the disappearing tissue-paper balls. Simply by asking a member of the audience to blow on his hands, the magician would make ball after ball vanish. Although Slydini repeated the trick over and over, the spectator would have no idea how he was doing it!

▶ *Tony Slydini was a master of what is known as ‘close-up magic’.*

Magical clock

★★★★ ★★★

Not only do you tell a person the number that they are thinking about, but you also predict which playing card they will pick!

Props needed...
* Pack of playing cards
* Paper
* Pencil

Preparation

• Secretly write on a piece of paper 'You will think of the ten of Hearts'. On the other side of the paper, draw a large round clock, including the numbers 1 to 12.

• Take out the ten of Hearts from your pack and put two pencil dots on the back of it in the top left and bottom right corners. Put this card back in the pack, 13th from the top.

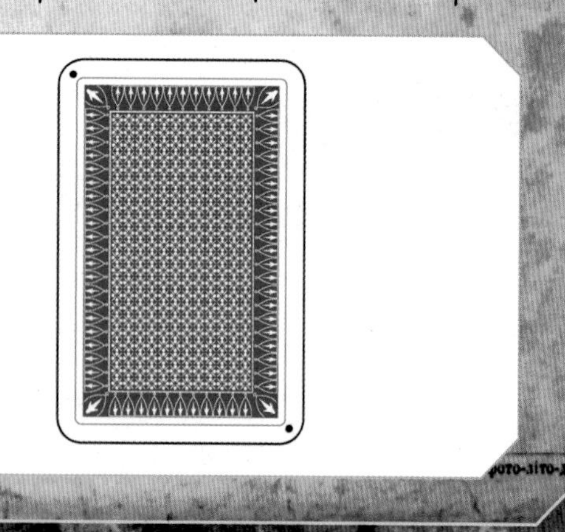

1 Show the clock to your friend and ask them to think of one of the numbers from 1 to 12. They should take out the same number of cards from the top of the pack and sit on them! Turn your head away so that you cannot see how many cards they take.

Top Tip!

This impressive trick deserves every bit of acting you can come up with. Make it look very difficult. It isn't, but that is no reason for you not to take credit for great skill, is it?

2

Say, “I need 12 cards”, and count off the top 12 cards, one at a time, then stack them into a little pile. This reverses the order of the cards and is important. Put the other cards aside.

3

Starting at one o’clock, go around the clock and put a card beside each number. As you do this, watch out for your card with the pencil dots in the corners. This will land on the number that your friend is thinking about! Let’s assume that it lands at six o’clock.

4

Say to your friend, “Please think of your number.” After a few seconds, say, “You are thinking of the number six and you are sitting on six cards! Am I right?” Then say, “Let’s see what card lies at six o’clock.” Turn it over to show the ten of Hearts. Then remove all the other cards from the clock and turn over the piece of paper. Your friend will read “You will think of the ten of Hearts.” Amazing!

▶ *Dai Vernon was one of the few people who could trick the famous Harry Houdini with a card trick.*

Fooling Houdini

Magician Dai Vernon (1894–1992) was known as the ‘professor’. He was perhaps the most skilful playing-card magician in the history of magic. He even fooled the great Houdini when he performed his trick the ‘Ambitious Card’. He repeated the trick eight times and still Houdini could not work out what Vernon was doing!

Coin in pocket

This is one of the most beautiful and graceful coin vanishing tricks used by magicians. It looks simple, but needs lots and lots of practice to make it look convincing to your audience.

Props needed...
* Large coin
* Handkerchief
* Jacket or shirt with a top breast pocket

1 Show your audience the coin you are holding in your left-hand fingertips. Your arm should be stretched out a bit.

2 Drape the handkerchief over the coin, but keep hold of the handkerchief with your right hand.

Top Tip!

Find a brightly coloured handkerchief with which to perform the trick. To make your act look really professional, iron the handkerchief thoroughly beforehand!

3 Pull the handkerchief across the coin and back towards your breast pocket. The coin can be seen again.

4 Repeat the action, but this time, as the handkerchief covers the coin, steal it away by gripping it between your right thumb and first finger. The handkerchief will hide the coin from view. Keep your left hand stretched out as if it still holds the coin.

5 Keep the handkerchief moving backwards towards your breast pocket.

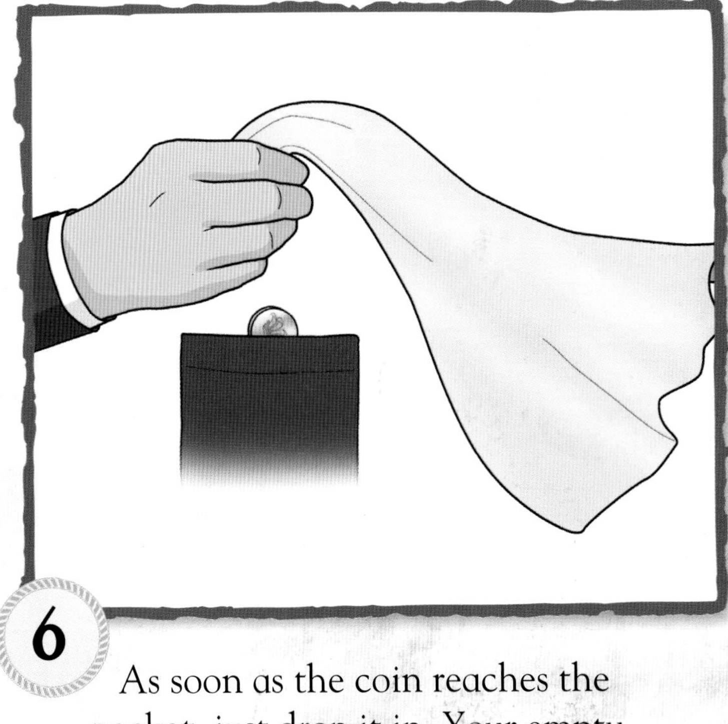

6 As soon as the coin reaches the pocket, just drop it in. Your empty left hand now comes into view. The coin has gone! Toss the handkerchief into the air and show that both of your hands are empty. The coin has completely disappeared!

Elastic arm

How can you make your left arm 30 centimetres longer than your right arm? Just as quickly, you change it back to its normal length again, of course!

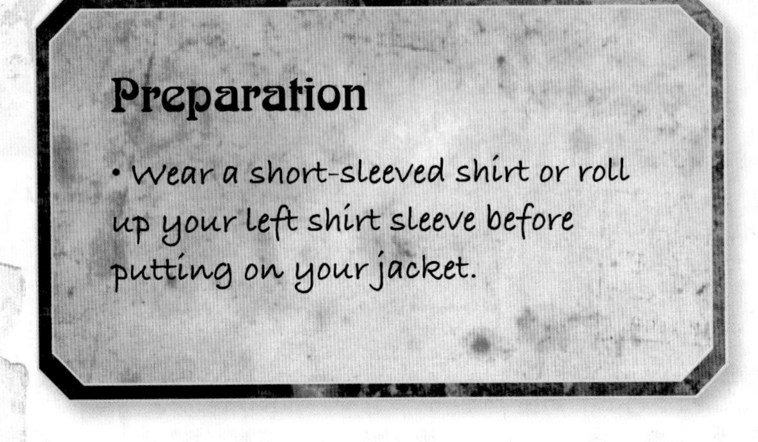

Preparation

• Wear a short-sleeved shirt or roll up your left shirt sleeve before putting on your jacket.

1 Hold your left arm across your body, pressing it to your chest all the time.

2 Now reach over with your right hand and grab your left wrist and pull it sideways. The hand, of course, moves, but the jacket sleeve stays where it was because it is trapped between your left arm and your chest.

3 The illusion of your arm stretching works really well. Try it out in front of a mirror. You can pretend to make your arm shorter again by twisting and pushing it back, still keeping your sleeve trapped as before.

PAPER TRICKS

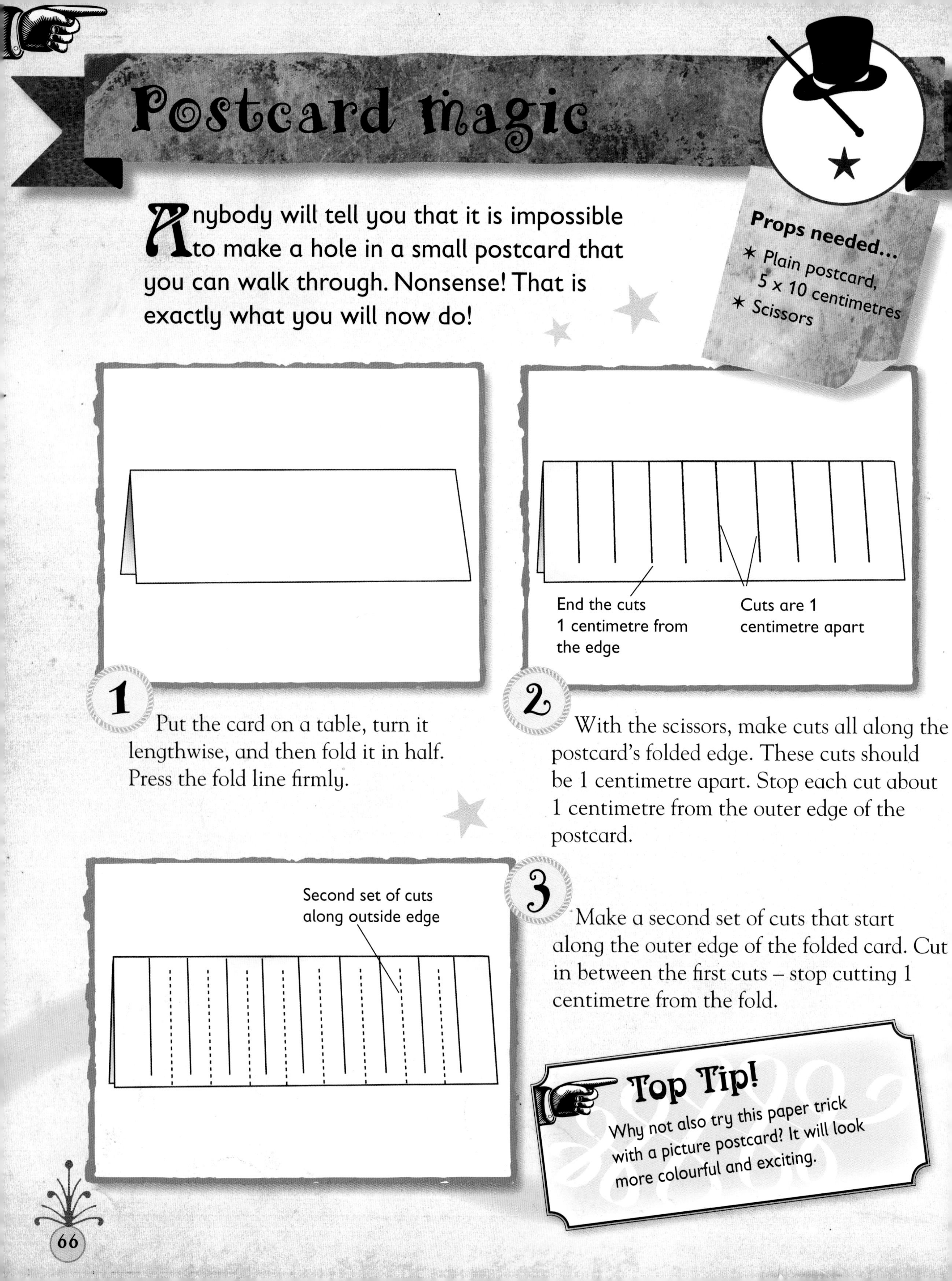

Postcard magic

Anybody will tell you that it is impossible to make a hole in a small postcard that you can walk through. Nonsense! That is exactly what you will now do!

Props needed...

* Plain postcard, 5 x 10 centimetres
* Scissors

1 Put the card on a table, turn it lengthwise, and then fold it in half. Press the fold line firmly.

2 With the scissors, make cuts all along the postcard's folded edge. These cuts should be 1 centimetre apart. Stop each cut about 1 centimetre from the outer edge of the postcard.

3 Make a second set of cuts that start along the outer edge of the folded card. Cut in between the first cuts – stop cutting 1 centimetre from the fold.

Top Tip!

Why not also try this paper trick with a picture postcard? It will look more colourful and exciting.

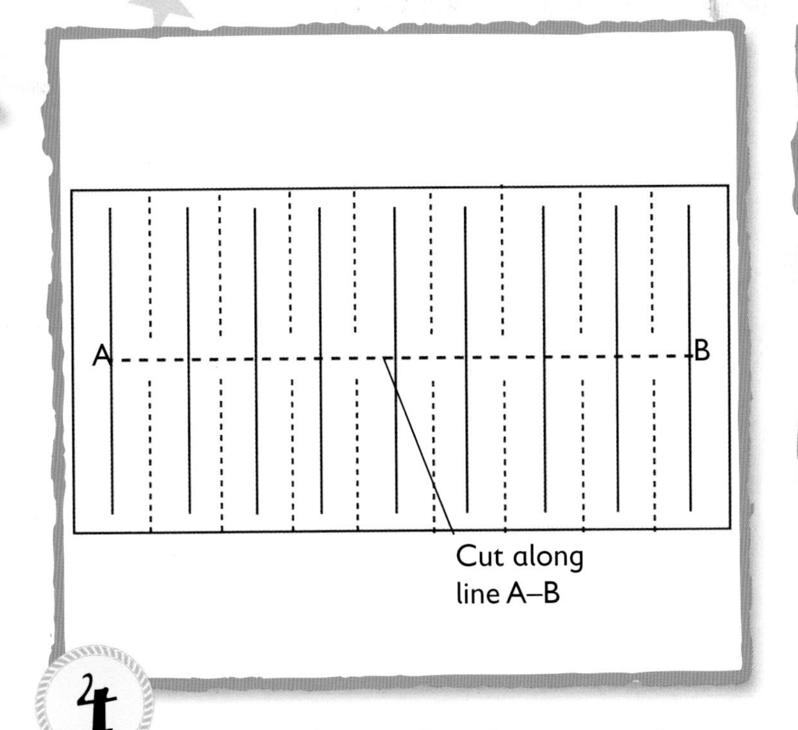

4 Open up the card and cut exactly along line A–B with the scissors.

5 When you have made all the cuts, gently open up the card into a big loop. This will be large enough for you to step through, carefully!

Salt Shaker

Dutch magician Fred Kaps (1926–1980) was most famous for a funny trick that he called the 'Salt Shaker'. Firstly, he poured a little salt onto his open hand and closed it. Suddenly, a long stream of salt came flowing out of this hand, which made a mess on the floor. Looking at the audience, Kaps pretended that he could not stop what was happening.

▶ *The 'Salt Shaker' was just one of Fred Kaps's many brilliant illusions. During his life, he was called the 'World's Greatest Magician'.*

Packets of money

Why not change a small coin into a much more valuable banknote? All you need are six square pieces of paper folded in a special way. The rest is magic!

Props needed...

* Two pieces of paper, each 15 x 15 centimetres
* Two pieces of paper, each 18 x 18 centimetres
* Two pieces of paper, each 21 x 21 centimetres
* Banknote and coin
* Pencil, ruler and glue

Preparation

1. On the two smallest pieces of paper, draw guidelines 4 centimetres from each edge. Then fold the right and left parts into the centre, and the top and bottom parts into the centre.

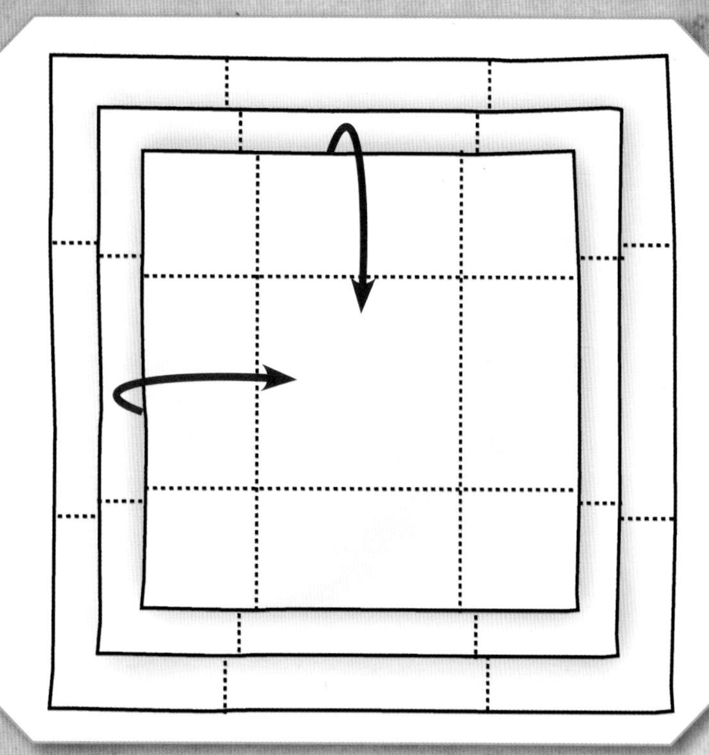

2. Repeat for the medium-sized pieces of paper, with the guidelines 5 centimetres from the edge.

3. Repeat for the large pieces of paper, with the guidelines 6 centimetres from the edge.

4. Take the two largest folded pieces of paper and stick them together, back to back, with glue.

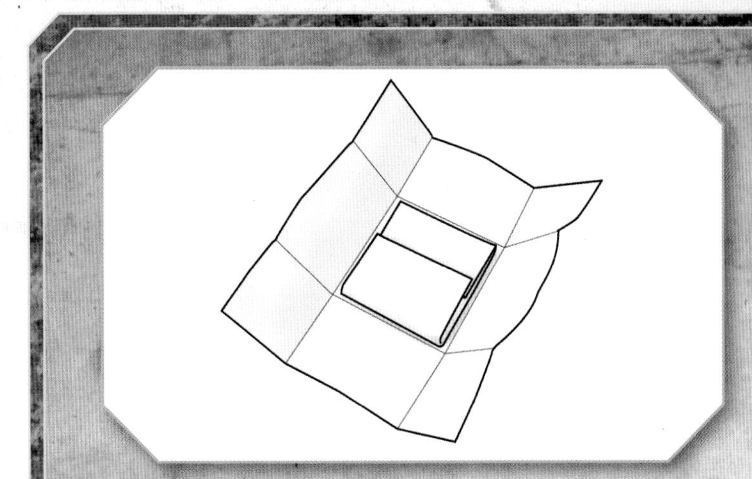

5. Put the smallest folded papers inside the middle-sized folded papers. Then, put these combined paper packets inside the largest packets. The packet now looks the same from the front or the back.

6. Unfold one side and secretly put a folded banknote in the centre. Refold the paper.

1 Open up the three papers from the side of the packet without the banknote and lay these on the table.

2 Let your audience see you put a small coin on the inside sheet. Then fold everything up again as it was before.

3 While you are pretending to press the folds together firmly, secretly turn the whole package over and lay it down on the table again.

4 Open up the paper and show your audience that the coin has changed into a banknote.

Boy meets girl

★★

How can you read some writing that is hidden behind your back? Simple! Your sensitive fingertips will do the reading for you!

Props needed...
* Plain postcard
* Pencil

Preparation

• Write the words 'BOY' and 'GIRL' on the postcard in capital letters. The spacing is important, so imagine the card is divided into nine sections. Each of the nine sections should have either 'BOY' or 'GIRL' written on it, as shown.

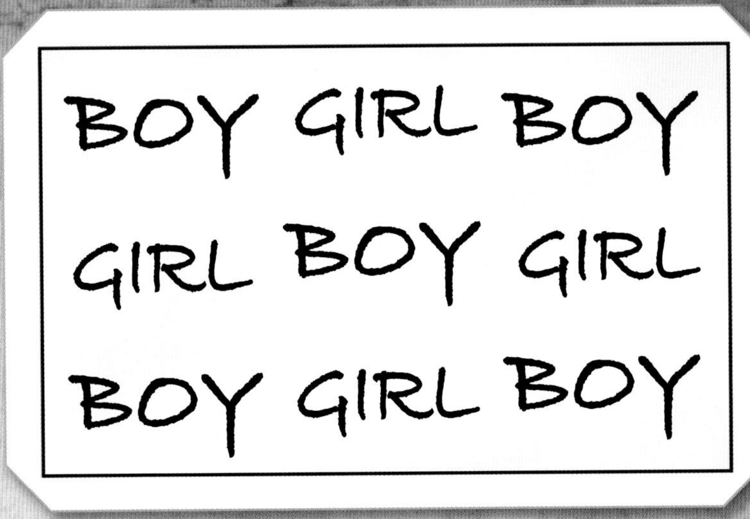

BOY GIRL BOY
GIRL BOY GIRL
BOY GIRL BOY

BOY GIRL BOY
GIRL BOY GIRL
BOY GIRL BOY

1 Tear up the postcard into the nine pieces. Give these to your friend and ask them to mix the pieces up.

2

Turn around, put your hands behind your back and ask your friend to place any one piece of card in your hands.

3

Then turn back to face your friend, still with your hands behind your back. Say, "I will try to read the name on this card with my fingertips. Yes, it reads 'BOY'." Bring the card out and show them that you are right.

3 rough sides = GIRL

2 rough sides + All rough sides = BOY

4

The secret is that you feel the edges of the card. If it has three rough edges and one smooth, untorn edge, it must be 'GIRL'. If the piece of card has two rough edges and two smooth ones, it must be 'BOY'. The centre piece has got four rough edges and this is also 'BOY'.

Top Tip!

Any set of two word pairs can be used in this trick. For example, 'cat' and 'mouse', 'chalk' and 'cheese', 'black' and 'white', 'fox' and 'hound', or 'dog' and 'bone'.

Memory skills

Magician Harry Lorayne is famous for his memory. As the audience of about 500 people arrive for one of his shows, Lorayne is told the name of each person once. An hour later, he asks the entire audience to stand up and says that he will name everyone. He will give $1,000 (about £600) to anyone he cannot name. Each person sits down once they are named. No-one is ever left standing!

▶ *Harry Lorayne's memory is incredible. It has to be; otherwise, he would not attempt some of his amazing tricks!*

Topsy-turvy money

★★

Props needed...
* Banknote

Turn a banknote upsidedown just by folding it from side to side. This crafty illusion works every time. Your friends will want to know how it's done!

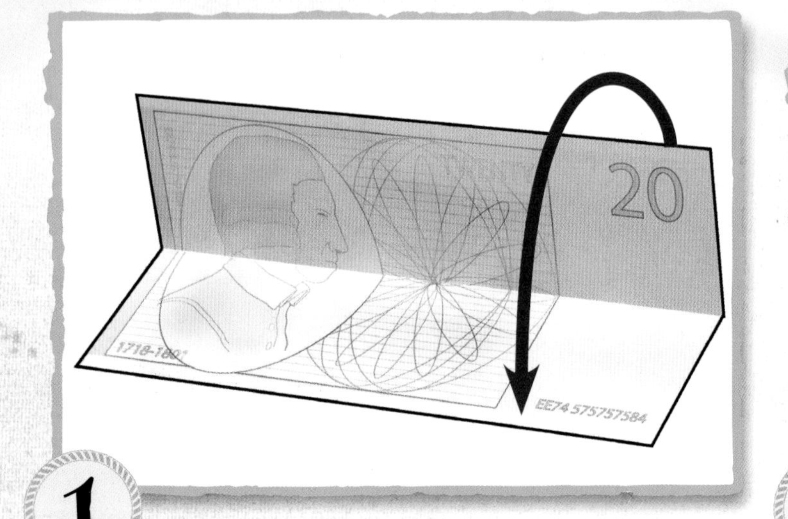

1 Lay the banknote on the table in front of you, lengthwise. Then fold the top half down.

2 Fold the banknote in half again, this time from left to right.

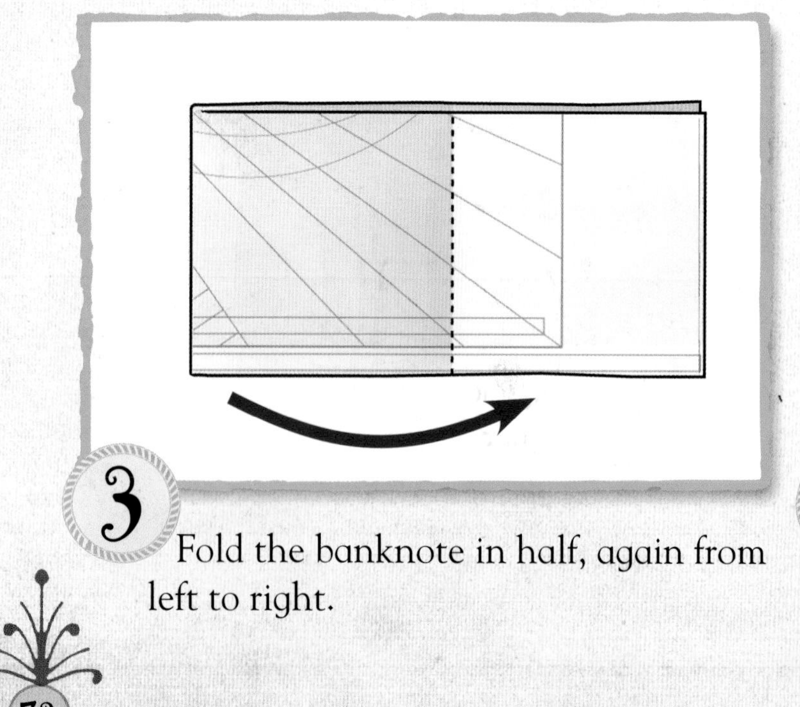

3 Fold the banknote in half, again from left to right.

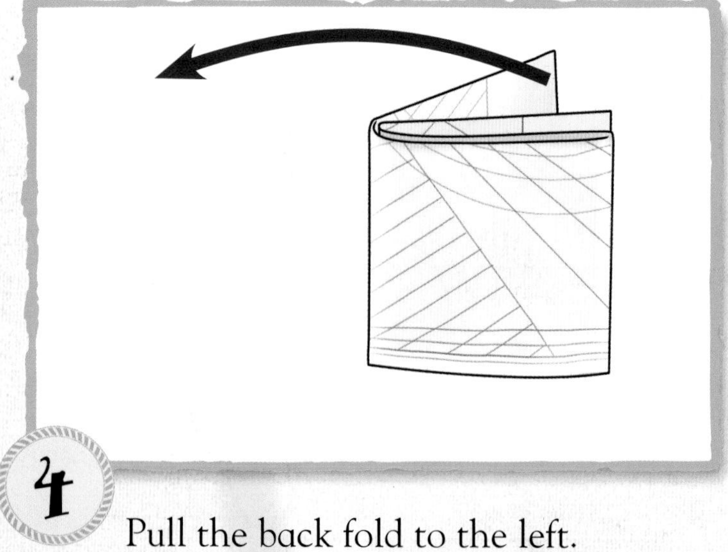

4 Pull the back fold to the left.

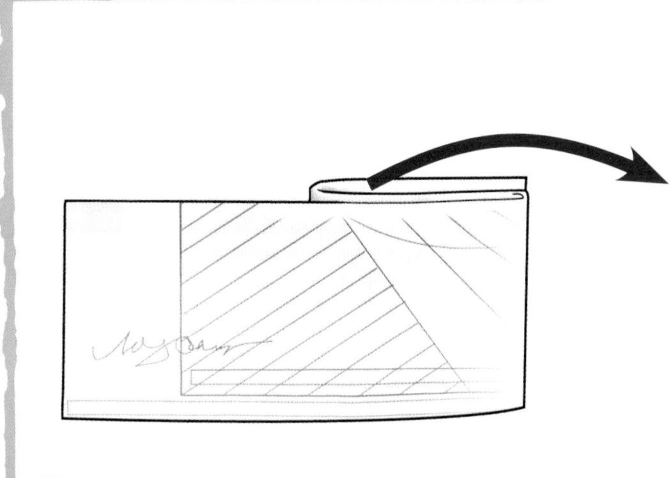

5 Now pull out the next back fold to the right.

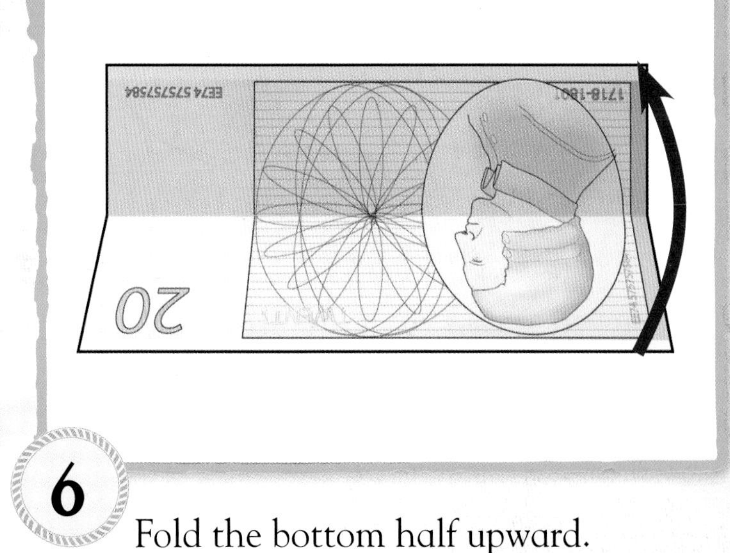

6 Fold the bottom half upward.

Mr Electric

Magician Marvyn Roy performed a dazzling magic act using only light bulbs. The act was called 'Mr Electric'. In one of these tricks, the magician pulled a never-ending string of glowing miniature light bulbs from his mouth. Later on, his wife leaped out of a gigantic light bulb during a trick called 'Girl in a Light Bulb'!

► *For more than 50 years, Marvyn Roy and his wife, Carol Roy, performed their light-bulb show around the world.*

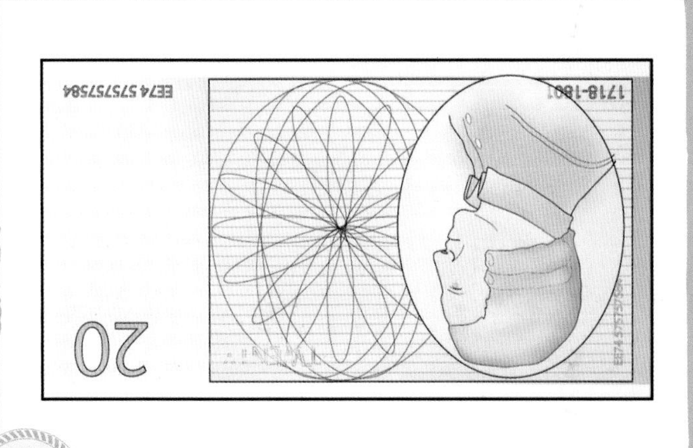

7 Mysteriously, the banknote has turned itself upside down!

Top Tip!

If you don't have a banknote, you can still perform the trick with a photograph that you have cut out from a magazine.

Instant tree

Using just a few pages from a magazine, you can make a 3-metre-high paper tree. This looks amazing when you pull it up from a small tube during a magic show!

Props needed...

* Eight sheets from a colour magazine. Remove the staples
* Scissors
* Sticky tape
* Pencil

1

Take the first sheet from the colour magazine and roll it into a tube.

2

Take the second sheet and place it so that it overlaps the end of the first sheet by about 5 centimetres. Continue rolling the tube.

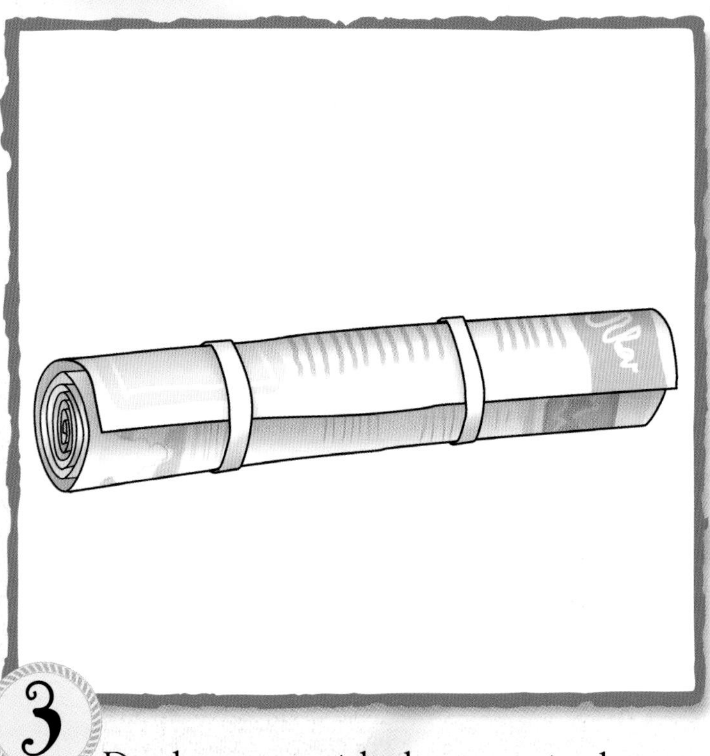

3

Do the same with the next six sheets from the magazine. Put a couple of strips of sticky tape across the last sheet to stop the tube from unrolling.

4 Make a cut about 10 centimetres long in one end of the tube. Then make another five cuts. These cuts should be spaced evenly around the tube. Mark their position with a pencil first.

5 Gently fold all of the flaps outward and downward.

6 Put your fingers inside the tube and slowly pull out the paper tree. As the tree grows, you will have to lie it on its side to pull it out. Once you have pulled it as far as it will go, you can stand the tree up.

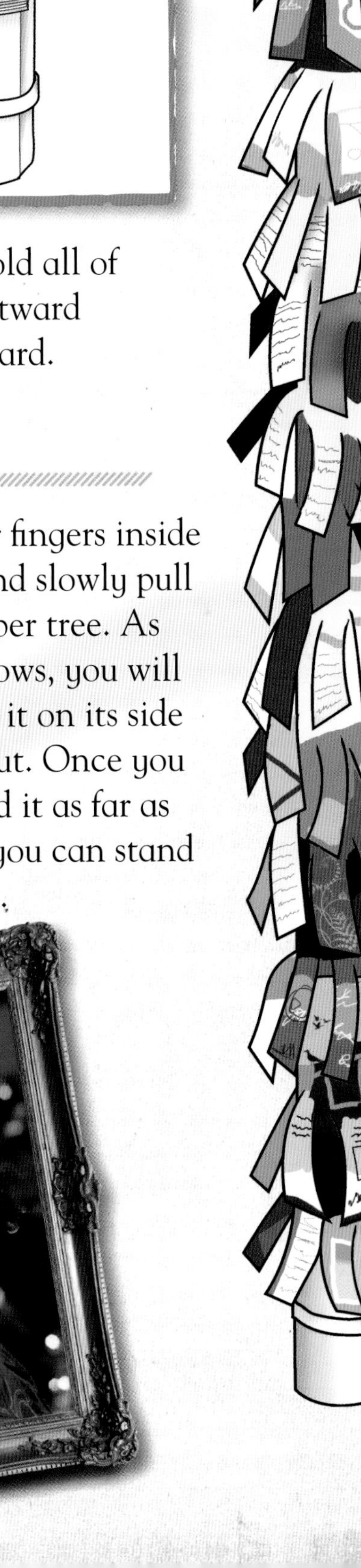

Shriek of Araby

William Oliver Wallace (1929–2009) was better known by his stage name, Ali Bongo. For his comedy magic act, which he titled the 'Shriek of Araby', he dressed in an oriental costume with gold, curly-toed slippers and a combined fez and turban. One of his best tricks featured a large silver ball that flew around the stage. To make it stop, the magician had to bash it with a mallet!

▶ *Before he became a full-time magician, Ali Bongo was manager of the magic department in London's famous Hamleys toy shop.*

Raise the ladder

★★★

How do you make a long ladder from a few pages of a colour magazine? Simple. All you need is sticky tape and a pair of scissors.

Props needed...
* Eight sheets from a colour magazine
* Scissors
* Sticky tape

1 Take the first sheet from the colour magazine and roll it into a tube. Take the second sheet and place it so that it overlaps the end of the first sheet by about 5 centimetres. Continue rolling the tube.

2 After you have rolled the final sheet from the magazine, use sticky tape to stop the sheets from unrolling.

3 Use the scissors to cut out a 10-centimetre long section from the centre of the tube. Flatten the tube slightly to make it easier for you to cut through the many layers of paper.

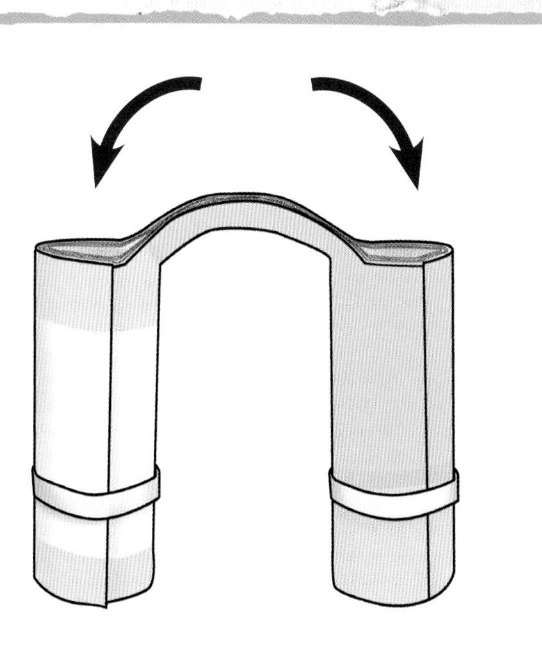

4 Press the tube to make it round again, and fold down the two ends.

5 Put your fingers in the centre of each tube and gently pull the paper out. Do this slowly, keeping the two sides even.

6 Keep pulling the rolled tubes until the paper ladder has been fully formed.

Magic all around

Much admired Richard 'Cardini' Pitchford (1895–1973) may be the most copied magician of all time. He performed a magical show in which strange things appeared to take place all around him. He pretended that he was as surprised as the audience about this, and that he could not stop what was happening.

◀ *Using simple props, such as billiard balls or playing cards, Cardini captivated his audiences in the world's largest theatres.*

Celebrity spotting

Ask five friends to write down secretly the name of a famous person they would like to be. In this trick, you will tell each friend who they have chosen.

Props needed...

* Five envelopes
* Five pencils
* Five pieces of paper

Preparation

• Mark four envelopes with a small pencil dot. Make these dots faint enough so that your friends will not notice them. The place where you put each dot will help you to tell which envelope is which. You do not have to mark the fifth envelope.

• Stack the envelopes in order, with the number one envelope on top. The fifth envelope, with no dot, is at the bottom.

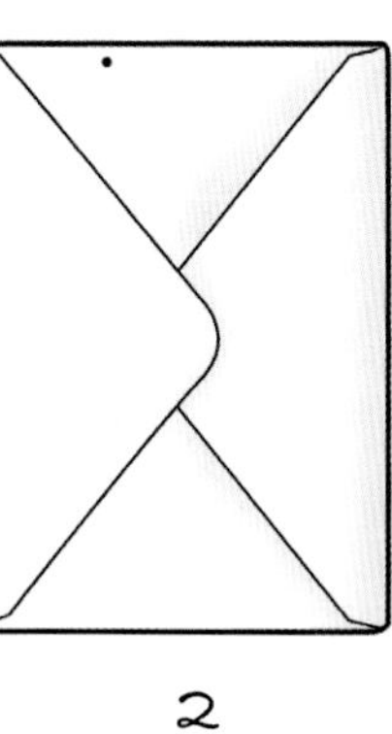
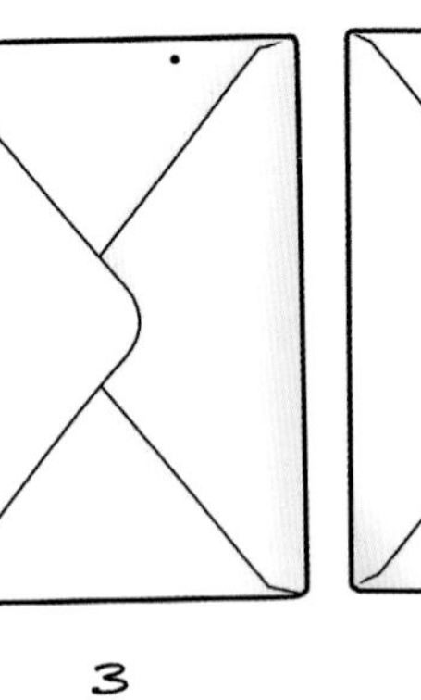
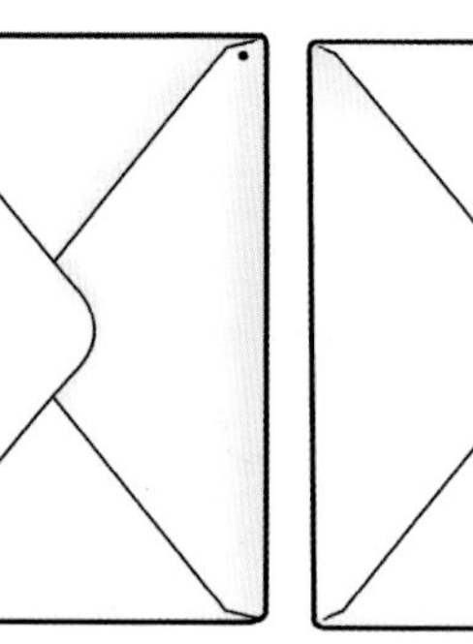
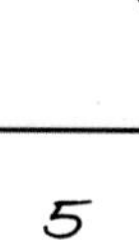

1 2 3 4 5

1

Hand out the envelopes to five friends in the order in which they are stacked. Give each person a pencil and paper and ask them to write down the name of someone famous they would like to be. Say that they should change their handwriting. Ask them to put the paper in the envelope and seal it.

2

Ask one of your friends to collect the envelopes and shuffle them before giving them back to you.

3

Pick up an envelope and look for your secret mark as you open it. This will tell you whose envelope it is. If 'Barack Obama' is written on the piece of paper, say, for example, "Barack Obama, I wonder who thought of him." Look at each person, then put your hand on the correct person's shoulder. "It's got to be you!" Repeat this with the second envelope.

4

Open the third envelope and take out the paper. Let's say it reads 'Robbie Williams'. Tell your three friends that you will do a lie detector test. They must all answer 'no' to your question. Hold the slip up in front of each of them in turn and say, "Do you want to be Robbie Williams?" You already know whose slip it is by the secret mark on the envelope, so you can pretend to know who is lying when they say 'no'!

5

Open the last two envelopes. Read out both names and return the slips to the right person.

Top Tip!

Use your acting skills to make this trick seem complicated. You must make it look as if you are finding it difficult to match the right name with the right person.

Newspaper cuttings

Take a strip of newspaper, fold it over and cut it in half. Then trim a bit more off. When you unfold it, the newspaper is one complete strip again. How is this done?

Props needed...

* Strip of newspaper, 5 x 50 centimetres
* Scissors
* Rubber cement
* Talcum powder

Preparation

• Spread some rubber cement across the centre of the newspaper strip. The cement should cover a patch 5 x 5 centimetres. Leave it to dry.

• Sprinkle talcum powder over the cement. Blow away any loose powder.

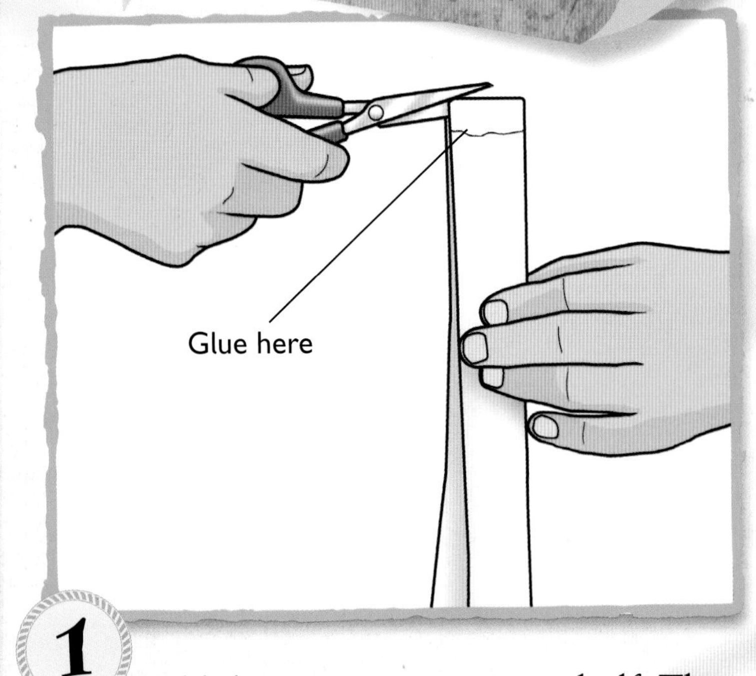

1 Fold the newspaper strip in half. The area with rubber cement should be on the outside of the folded strip. Take the scissors and cut the strip in half through the fold in the centre.

Top Tip!

Make sure that the strip of newspaper you use does not have photographs or bold headings. These may make the cuts more obvious to your audience.

2 Show your audience the two strips of newspaper, holding one in each hand.

3 Bring the two newspaper strips together. Make sure that the areas you covered with rubber cement are on the inside, pressing against each other.

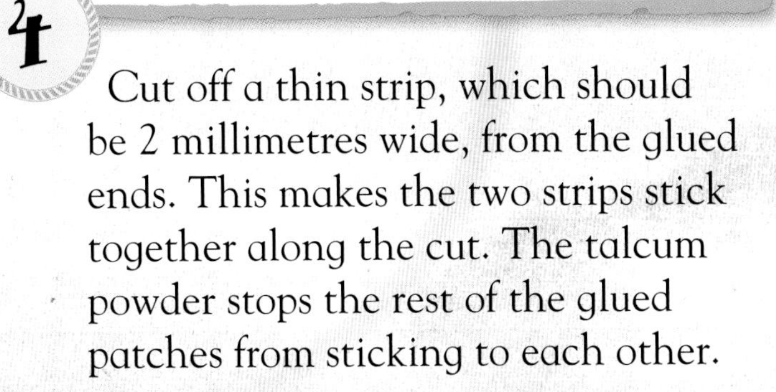

4 Cut off a thin strip, which should be 2 millimetres wide, from the glued ends. This makes the two strips stick together along the cut. The talcum powder stops the rest of the glued patches from sticking to each other.

5 Finally, let one end of the newspaper strip drop down. The two newspaper strips are now one piece again.

Magic cone

Put together this clever cone and you can make coins and other small objects vanish into thin air with a wave of your magic wand.

Props needed...

* Large sheet of cardboard
* Scissors
* Colourful sticky tape
* Pencil and ruler
* Coin
* Magic wand

Preparation

• Draw three triangles on the cardboard. These triangles are joined together. The longest sides of the triangles are 25 centimetres long. You can copy the 45-degree angles from this book. Cut out the complete shape. Then draw just a triangle A shape and cut this out as well.

B A C A
45 degrees
45 degrees
45 degrees
25 centimetres
25 centimetres

C B A

C B A

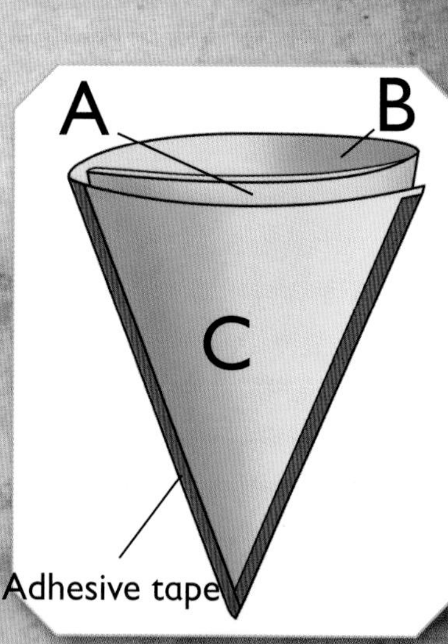

• Put the single triangle A on top of the other triangle A, and then stick it down with sticky tape. Do this along the two longest sides. This forms a secret pocket.

• Put sticky tape along the join between triangles B and C, and along the outside edge of C. Do the same on the other side of the cardboard so that both sides look the same.

• With the second triangle A on top, fold triangle A over triangle B. Then fold triangle C over triangle B. Press all the folds down firmly.

1 Open up the complete cone and show your friend both sides. Then fold it up again to remake the cone.

2 Gently squeeze the sides of the cone and the secret pocket will open a little. Drop a coin into the secret pocket.

3 Tap the cone with your magic wand. Open up the cone and show your friend that the coin has vanished.

4 When making the coin come back, first open up the cone and show your friend that it is empty. Then fold in the sides and shake out the coin. Make sure that your friend does not see the opening of the secret pocket.

Top Tip!

You can load all sorts of flat things into your secret pocket. These could include small silk handkerchiefs, folded banknotes, postage stamps or streamers.

White rabbits

You can also use your magic cone to pull out white rabbits. As you reveal each one, give it to someone in your audience.

Props needed...

* Twenty pieces of white paper, each 10 x 10 centimetres
* Scissors
* Pencil

Preparation

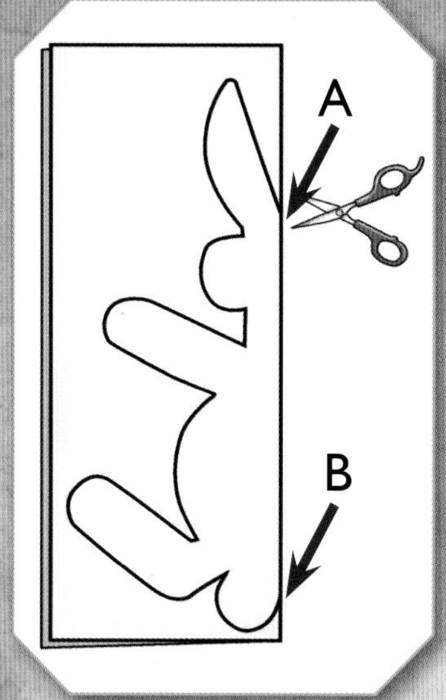

1. Fold a sheet of paper in half and draw the outline of a rabbit. Cut out the rabbit, starting at point A and ending at B.

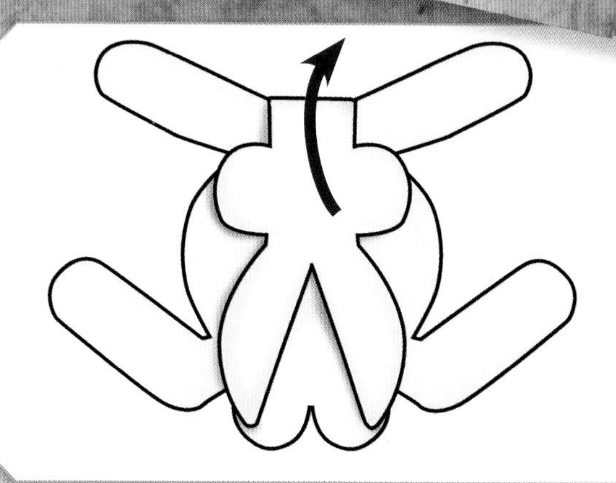

2. Open up the paper rabbit and fold its head and neck down.

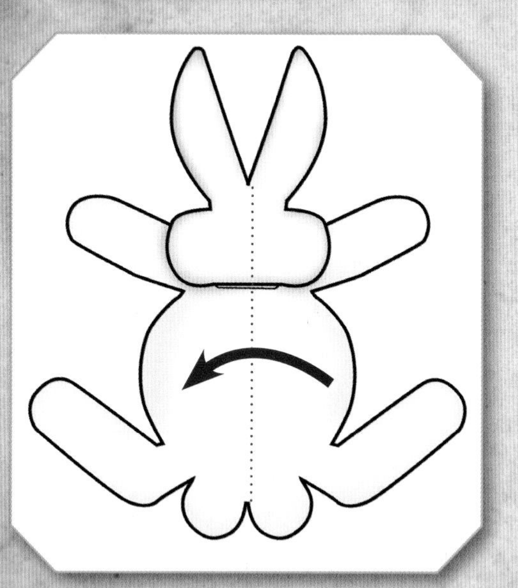

3. Now fold up just the head. Do not fold up the neck.

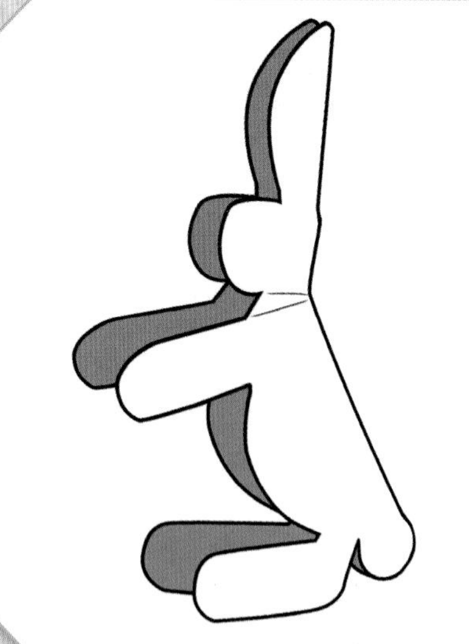

4. Fold the rabbit in half lengthwise and pull its head back a little. Press the creases down and push up the tail.

5. Make twenty rabbits and put them into the magic cone's secret pocket.

Top Tip!

You can decorate each paper rabbit by drawing an eye on each side of the head. This will make the rabbit even more cute!

1 Make sure that you open up the cone and show your audience that the cone is empty. They will not be able to see the rabbits hidden in the secret pocket.

2 Fold in the flaps and wave your magic wand over the cone.

3 Start pulling out the rabbits one at a time. Your friends will be amazed, as there seems to be a never-ending line of rabbits for them to keep.

Pick a colour

Throw lots of small paper balls of different colours into a bag. Ask your friend to take one out and tell them that you know which colour they will choose. You will be right every time!

Props needed...

* Tissue paper in different colours
* Two paper bags of the same size
* Sticky tape
* Scissors
* Writing paper
* Pencil

Preparation

• Use the two paper bags to make a double bag. First, lay one bag over the other. Then, tape them together with sticky tape along the three unopened sides. Magicians call this prop a 'change bag'.

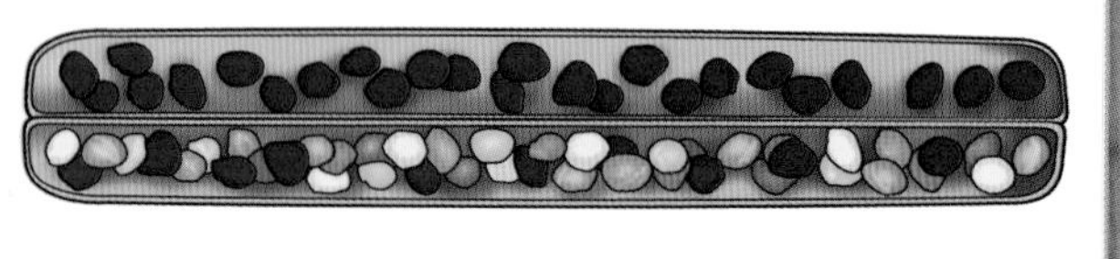

• Make 25 small red paper balls by screwing up small pieces of red tissue paper. Drop these into one side of the double bag. Then make 45 more paper balls in different colours. Ten of these 45 balls should be red. Put these in the other side of the double bag.

I know that you will choose a red ball

• Write 'I know that you will choose a red ball' on a piece of paper. Fold this and put it in your top pocket.

1

Hold the bag so that it is open and your friend can see the opening. Keep closed the secret section that contains only red balls. Tell your friend that you will let them reach into the bag to pick out a ball and that you know which colour they will choose.

2

Lift the bag to head height and change your grip so that only the secret section is open. Then roll the top of the bag down 2 centimetres. This will hide the double opening at the top.

3

Hold the bag up to your friend at head height and ask them to reach in and remove a ball, which they should show you. It will, of course, be red. Put the bag to one side.

4

Then say, "There is something I want to show you." Take out the note on which you have written 'I know that you will choose a red ball' from your pocket. Ask your friend to read it and watch the expression on their face!

Top Tip!

You can also make a change bag using see-through bags. As long as you keep the section that contains the red balls facing you during the trick, your friend will not see the second bag. They will only see the balls in the bag nearest to them.

Tear it up

Tear up some tissue paper and roll the pieces into a ball. Then, with a wave of your magic wand, amaze your audience as you fold out the ball and show a complete piece of tissue paper.

Props needed...

* Two pieces of tissue paper of the same colour, both 4 x 5 centimetres in size
* Magic wand

Preparation

- Put your magic wand in your right jacket pocket.
- Lay one piece of tissue paper on a table.
- Crush the other piece of tissue paper into a ball and hide it in your right hand.

Ball hidden here

1 Pick up the tissue paper on the table with your left hand. Grip it with your right thumb and first finger as well.

2 Tear the tissue paper in half. Then put one half on top of the other on the table. Turn these halves lengthwise and tear them through the centre again. Place all the pieces together and tear them in half again.

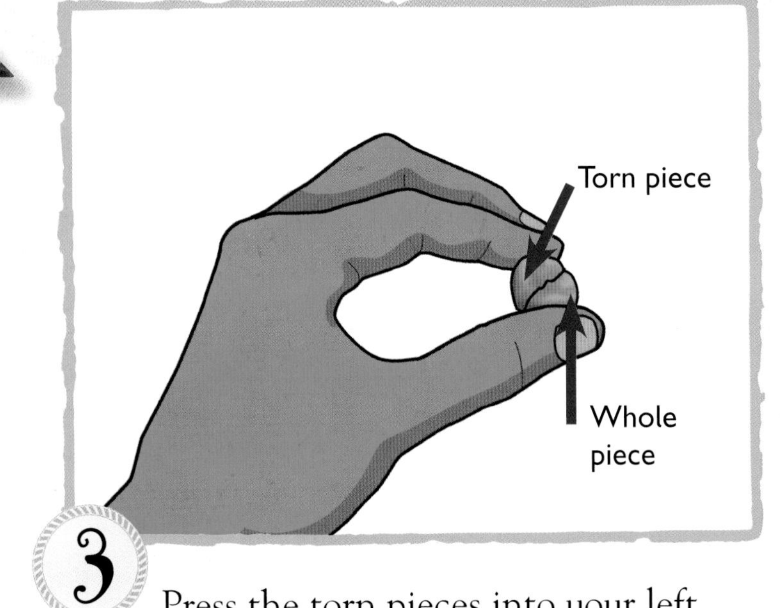

3 Press the torn pieces into your left hand and squash them into a ball. Secretly push this ball into the ball you have been holding in your right hand. Then hold these between your left thumb and first finger so that they look like one ball.

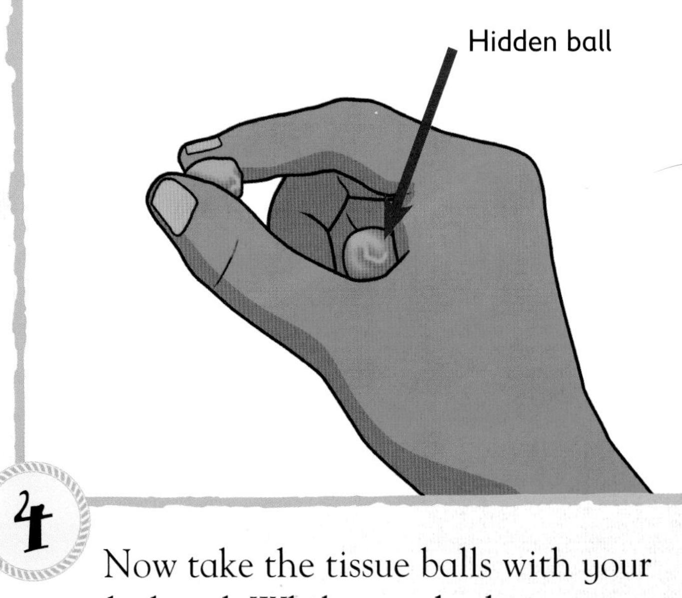

4 Now take the tissue balls with your right hand. While you do this, turn your right hand a little. This will help you to hide the ball made of torn pieces behind your second, third and fourth fingers.

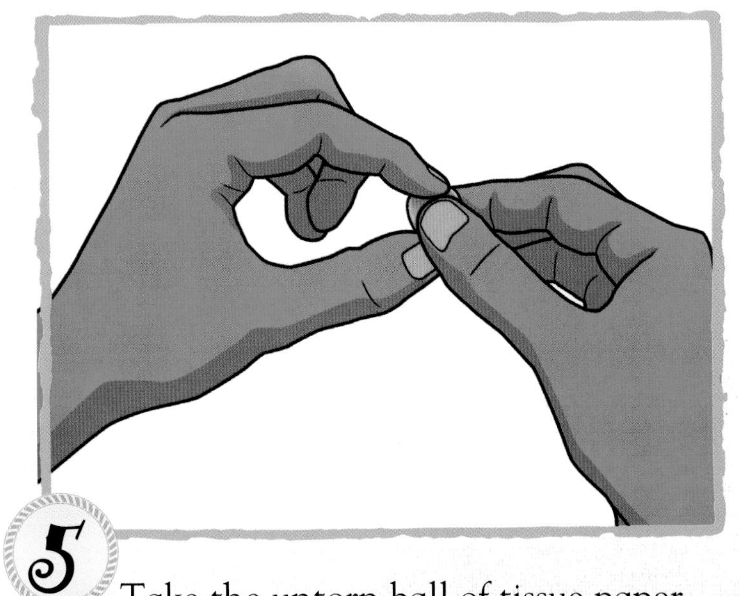

5 Take the untorn ball of tissue paper with your left hand. At the same time, put your right hand in your right jacket pocket and put the torn ball there. Leave the torn pieces in your pocket and bring out your magic wand.

6 Tap the ball of tissue in your hand with the wand. Then fold out the ball to show that it has been magically restored and the tissue paper is no longer torn.

Paper money

Why not amaze your friends by making folded banknotes come tumbling out of a folded sheet of newspaper! All you need to do is to make a secret paper pocket.

Props needed...

* Two identical sheets of newspaper, each with a photograph near the top, right-hand corner. The photograph should be 12 centimetres long by two columns wide
* Pretend banknotes
* Scissors
* Glue

Preparation

• Cut out the photograph from one newspaper sheet. Put a line of glue around three sides and stick it on the same photograph in the other sheet. The open side faces the centre of the newspaper to make a secret pocket.

• Fold lots of the pretend banknotes into quarters and slide them into the secret pocket. Keep everything as flat as possible.

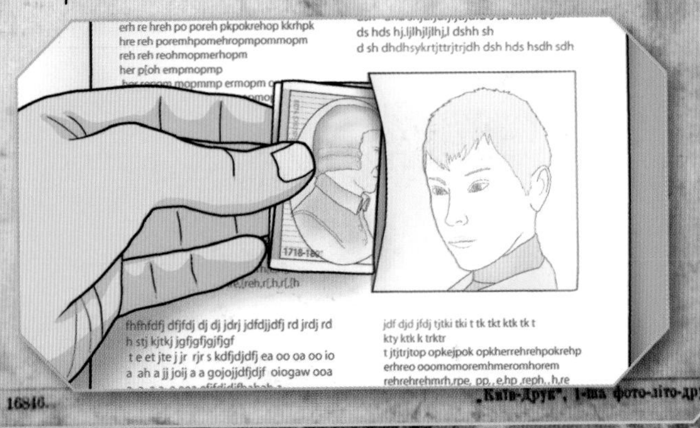

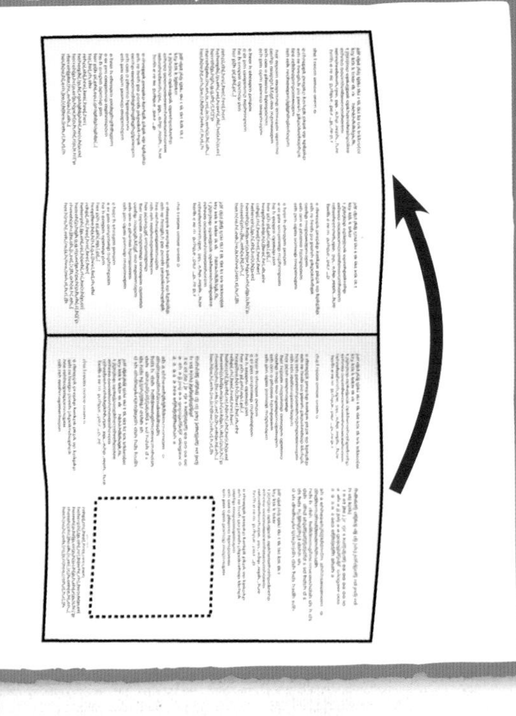

1 Open up the newspaper sheet and lay it on a table. The secret pocket should be facing down in the bottom left corner.

2 Carefully pick up the newspaper sheet by the other end.

3 Turn the newspaper around to show the other side.

4 Quickly reach down and bring the lower edge of the newspaper to the top. As you do this, the folded banknotes will drop out of the secret pocket and into the centre crease.

5 Tip the banknotes out onto the table with a flourish!

Top Tip!

You could produce lots of other flat things from the newspaper instead of money – for example, postage stamps. If your pocket was big enough, you could even magic a CD from it!

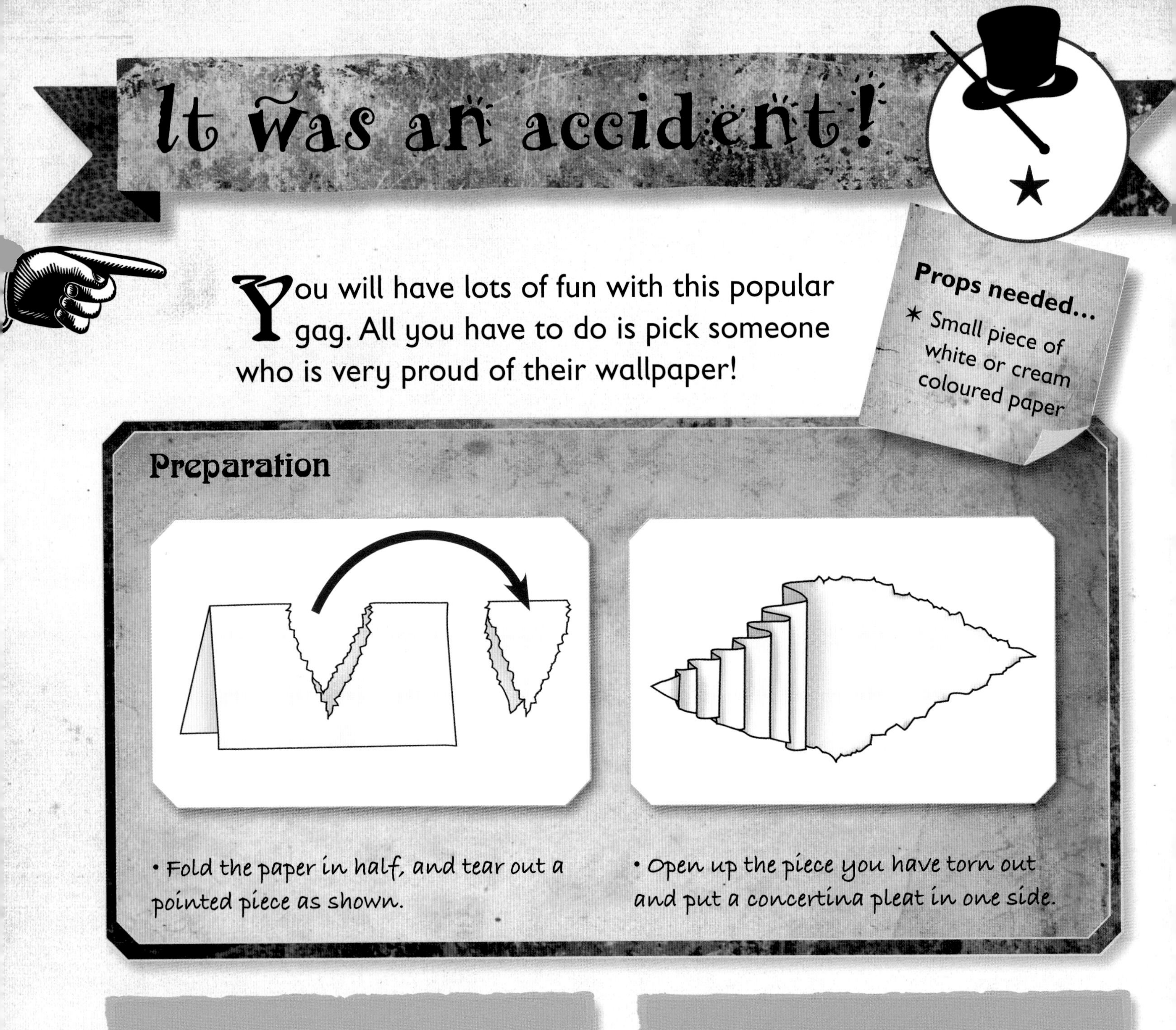

It was an accident!

You will have lots of fun with this popular gag. All you have to do is pick someone who is very proud of their wallpaper!

Props needed...

* Small piece of white or cream coloured paper

Preparation

• Fold the paper in half, and tear out a pointed piece as shown.

• Open up the piece you have torn out and put a concertina pleat in one side.

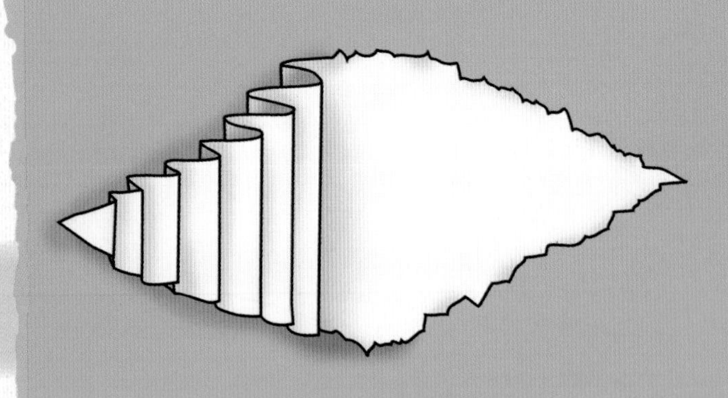

1

Moisten the back of the other side. Then press the piece onto a wall that is decorated with coloured wallpaper.

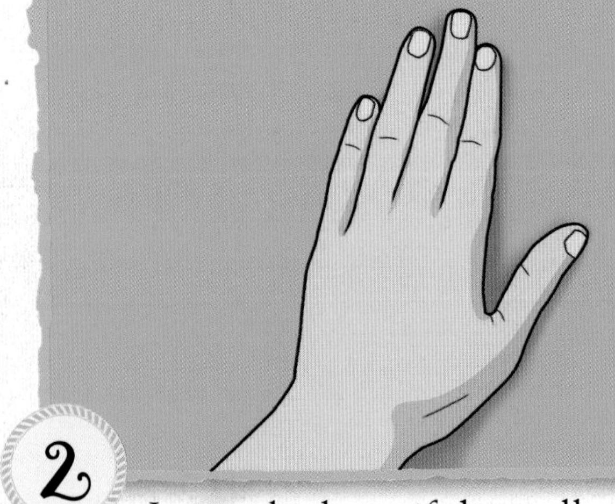

2

It now looks as if the wallpaper has been ripped! Offer to restore the wallpaper by magic. Place your hand over the 'rip', rub the white paper off and all is back to normal.

MAGIC WITH NUMBERS

The $3\frac{1}{2}$ of Clubs

With just a playing card, an envelope and a die, you can ask your friend to give you a number and predict it correctly.

Props needed...

* Three of Clubs from an old pack of playing cards
* Black marker pen
* Small envelope
* Die

Preparation

• Take the black marker pen and write a '1/2' after each number 3 on the 3 of Clubs card. Also draw the extra half-club symbol.

• Insert the card into the envelope. Put the envelope and the die onto a table when you start the trick.

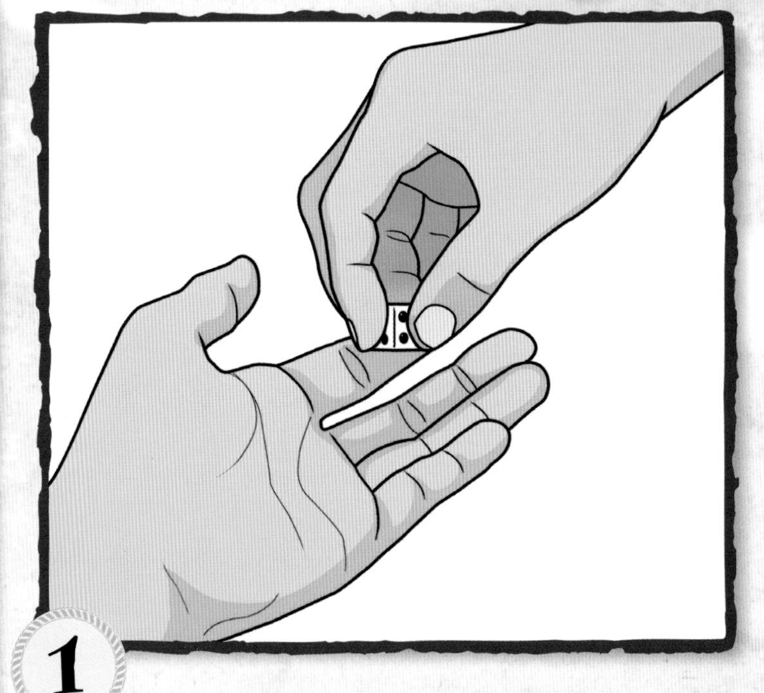

1 Say to your friend, "Inside this small envelope is a playing card. The number on this hidden card is the same as the one you are about to give me!" Then give your friend the die.

Top Tip!

The answer will always be $3\frac{1}{2}$, because the opposite sides of a die always total seven – 1 + 6 = 7, 2 + 5 = 7 and 3 + 4 = 7.

2

Say, "When my back is turned, I want you to roll the die. When it stops, add the number on the top of the die to the number on the bottom. Then divide this total by two." After a short pause, add, "The number of the playing card in the envelope will be the same as your total."

3

"Have you done that? What was your final total?" Your friend will say, "$3\frac{1}{2}$" and laugh, because they will think that they have caught you out. You should pretend to be upset. Then, slowly, pull out the $3\frac{1}{2}$ of Clubs from the envelope to show that you were right after all!

▼ *Sorcar performs his grisly illusion in London in 1956. Don't worry! It was an illusion – his female assistant was not harmed!*

Televized sensation

The great Indian magician P. C. Sorcar (1913–1971) caused a sensation in Britain when he performed an illusion live on television. His female assistant was laid on a table and a huge, rotating circular saw was lowered onto her middle. It appeared to slice her in two! Unfortunately, the live television broadcast ran out of time at this point. Millions of worried viewers were left wondering what had happened to her!

Domino trick

How can you predict which dominoes will be at the two ends of a line of dominoes? Especially as you won't be in the room when your friend lays them out!

Props needed...
* Domino set
* Envelope
* Paper and pencil

Preparation

• Secretly take one of the dominoes. For example, it could be a 6–1. Write on a piece of paper 'I predict that the two end numbers will be a one and a six.'

• Put the paper in an envelope and seal it. Place the envelope on a table with the set of dominoes before you start.

1 Put the dominoes out on a table so that they are all face up. Tell your friend to start matching up the dominoes in the same way as they would when playing a game of dominoes. That is, put a five-dots pattern against another five-dots pattern, and so on.

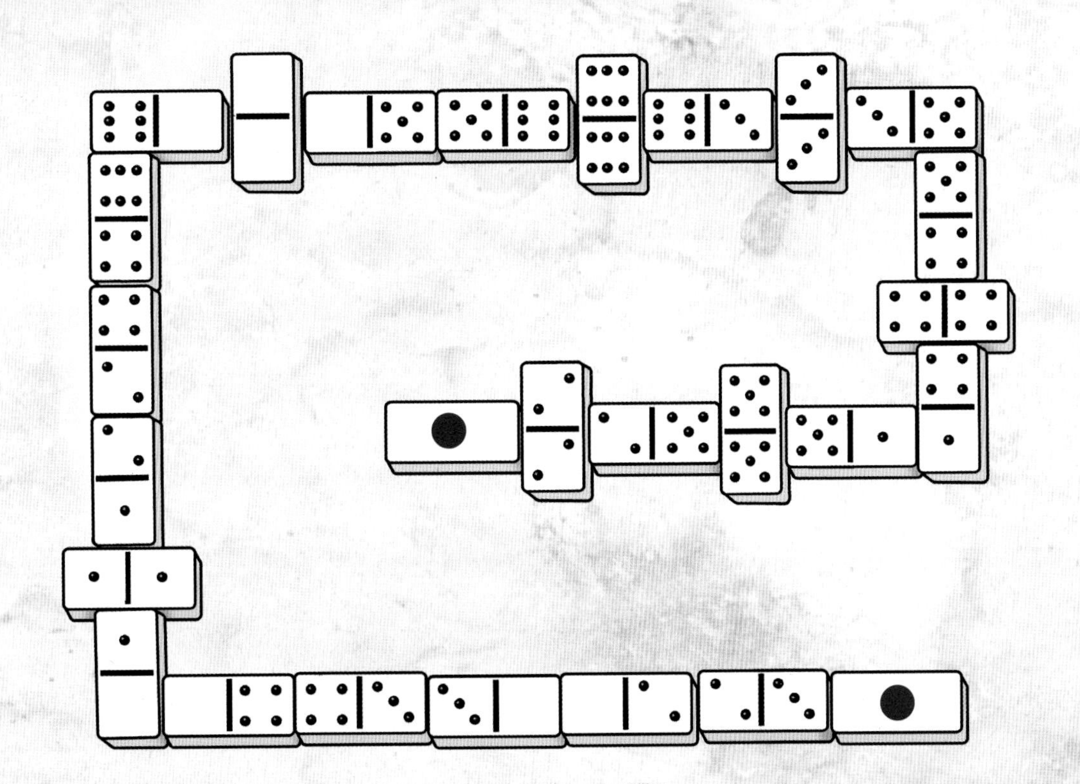

2 Before your friend starts joining the dominoes together, tell them that you will leave the room for a short while. Before you go, tell them that they should leave the dominoes at each end of the line face down. That way, when you come back into the room you won't be able to see what they are.

3 When you return, pretend to look at the dominoes on the table carefully. Then tell your friend the numbers on the face-down dominoes. In this example, they will be 3–1 and 2–6.

Top Tip!

You can repeat the trick by secretly replacing the domino that you had taken and stealing another one in its place! In this trick, the two end numbers in the domino spread will always be the same as the numbers on the domino you took away. It's magic!

4 Now ask your friend to open the envelope and read out your prediction. This will, of course, be correct!

Top and bottom

Props needed...
* Three dice

This is a great mind-reading trick that is based on a simple fact. That is, when added together, the top and bottom numbers of a dice always total seven.

1 Ask your friend to stack the three dice, one on top of another. Before they do this, turn your back to your friend so that you can't see the dice.

2 Give your friend enough time to make the stack. Then turn around for a split second and say, "Have you done that yet?" Immediately turn your head away again to make it seem that you did not see the dice. In this split second, look at the number at the top of the dice pile. Let's say it is a three.

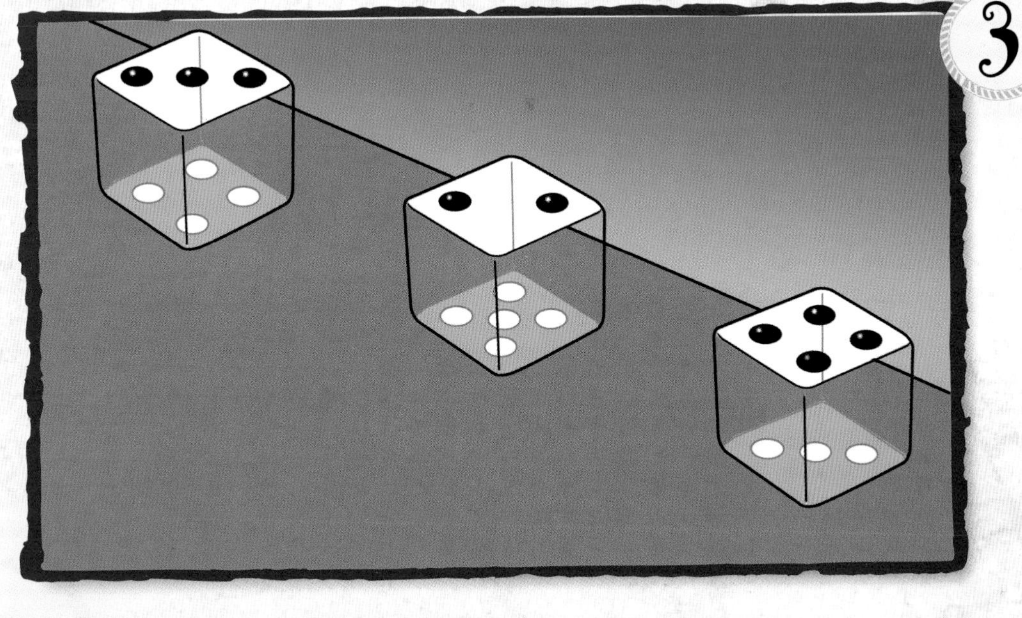

3 Then say, "There are five sides of the dice that you can't see – the one at the bottom and the four sides sandwiched between the dice. Look at these sides of the dice and add their numbers together. Don't say the total out loud; just think of the total."

Wait for a few seconds, then say, "You are thinking of the number 18." If the top number was three, you will be right!

Top Tip!

When added up, the top and bottom sides of a dice always total seven. Therefore, the top and bottom sides of three dice will always total 21. You just have to subtract the number that you secretly glimpsed from 21 to arrive at the correct answer.

Indian rope trick

Magician Howard Thurston (1869–1936), from Ohio in the United States, had the largest travelling magic show of his time. It took a train more than ten cars long to transport his props. Thurston featured the famous Indian rope trick. A rope is thrown up into the air, and stays there. A little boy then climbs to the top of a rope and vanishes!

◀ *The Indian rope trick was first performed in India in the 1800s.*

Speedy maths

★★★

Props needed...
* Pencil
* Paper

It is simple to do a difficult sum – you just have to know the secret formula. Your friends will think that you are a maths genius when you show them this numbers trick!

```
• • • • •
• • • • •
• • • • •
• • • • •
_________
199,998
```

1 Draw four rows of five dots on a piece of paper. Then draw a line beneath the dots to show that it is a sum. Fill in 199,998 under the line as the total.

```
76045
• • • • •
29283
• • • • •
_________
199,998
```

2 Ask your friends to fill in the first and third lines with any numbers that they wish. It is their choice. Let's suppose that they write 76,045 and 29,283.

Top Tip!

How do you know what numbers to use? All you do is write a number that, when added to the number above, will add up to nine. The first number in the top line is a seven, so under it you put a two. Next is a six, so you put a three, and so on. You also use this method with the fourth row. Easy!

3

Say that you will fill in the gaps with numbers to make the total correct. You will make things more difficult for yourself by starting from the left side – not the right side, which is the normal way of doing sums. You will do this in only 10 seconds!

76045
23954
29283
70716

199,998

4

After you have filled in your numbers, the sum looks like this. Your sum, of course, is correct.

Starting young

Hungary's most famous magician, Anikó Ungár, has performed her stunning magic shows all over the world. These have earned her many important prizes. After studying textile design at an early age, Anikó Ungár changed direction and went on to build a career as a magician. Encouraged by her father, who was an amateur magician, she learned her first tricks at the age of 13.

▶ *Anikó Ungár uses a wide variety of props during her stunning magic shows.*

Always 34

Props needed...
* Pencil
* Paper

This mathematical trick is totally baffling, but it works every time! It is easy to do. All you need is a pencil and a piece of paper on which you write the numbers 1 to 16.

Preparation

* Secretly write the number 34 on the back of the piece of paper.

1	2	3	4
5	6	7	8
9	10	11	12
13	14	15	16

1 Write the numbers 1 to 16 on the blank side of the piece of paper. Use the pattern shown here.

1	2	3	4
5	6	7	8
9	10	11	12
13	14	15	16

2 Ask your friend to say a number from 1 to 16. Let's pretend they choose number 11. Draw a circle around 11 and then the two lines through it, as shown.

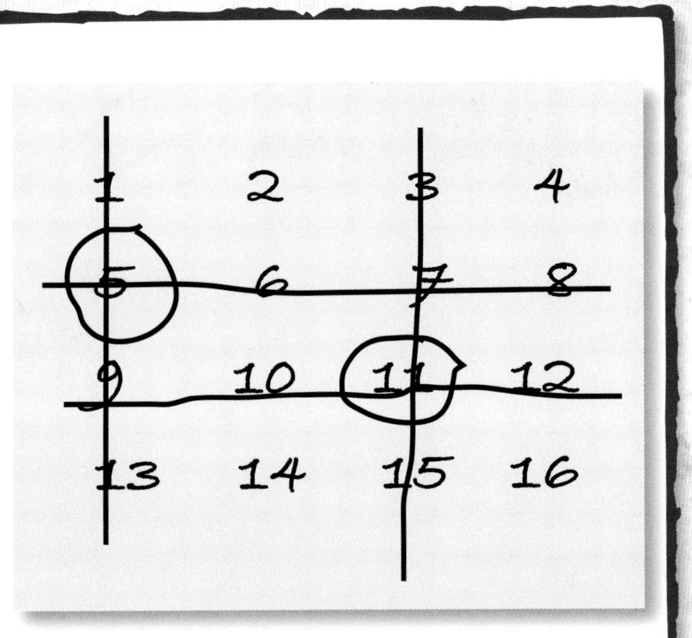

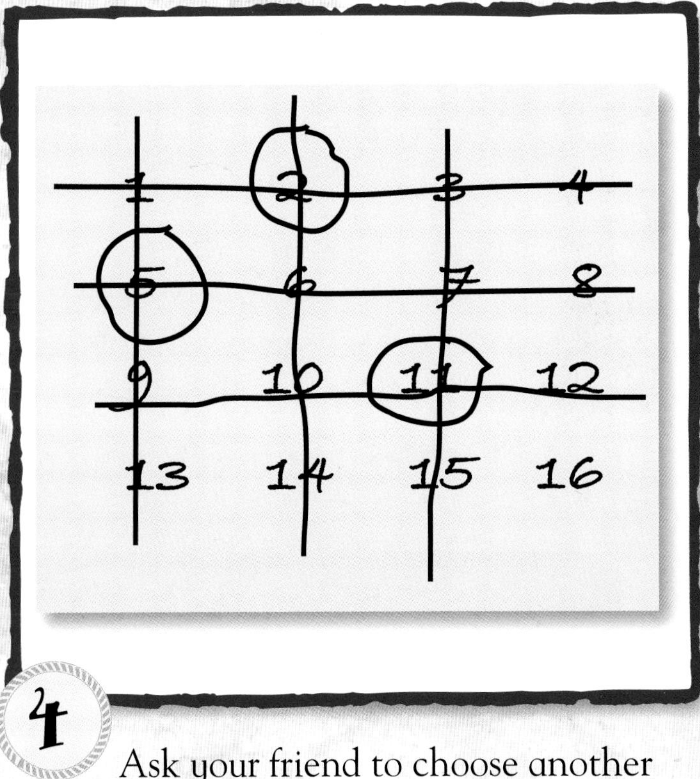

3

Show your friend the piece of paper. Ask them to choose another number that does not have a line through it. Let's assume they say 5. Cross this out both ways as you did with 11.

4

Ask your friend to choose another number that has not been crossed through. This time, let's pretend they say 2. Draw lines through this number, as you did before.

5

Only the number 16 has not been struck through. Ask your friend to add 16 to the three numbers they have already chosen. This is the sum:

16 + 11 + 5 + 2 = 34

Turn over the paper and show that you have already written 34!

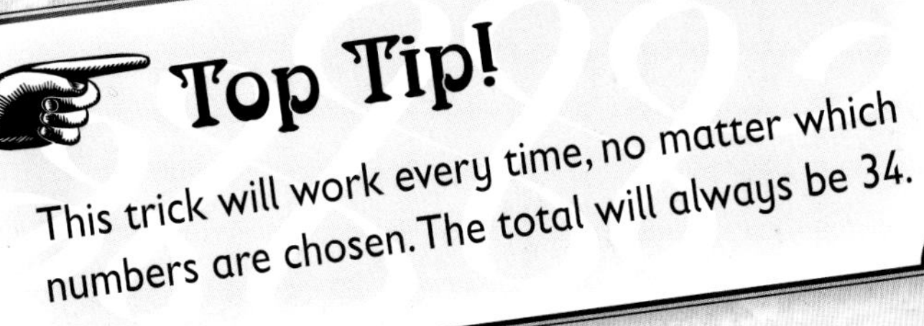

Question: Two rows of coins are laid out as shown. One row contains five coins; the other, four coins. By moving only one coin, how can you end up with two rows, each four coins long?

O O O O
O
O
O
O

Answer: Put two coins at the corner point, one on top of the other!

O O O O
O
O
O

Special number

The number 1089 is magical. Ask your friend to do a few sums, and the answer will be 1089! Your friend will think you have special powers when you predict the answer!

Props needed...

* Paper
* Pencil

Preparation

• Write the number 1089 on one side of the piece of paper.

1089

Floating light bulb

Harry Blackstone, Jnr (1934–1997) performed a brilliant trick with a light bulb. First he made the bulb light up in his hand. Then, the bulb floated around the stage, still lit. It then floated over the heads of the audience before returning to the magician's hand. With a wave of his hand, the lighted bulb finally disappeared!

▲ *Magician Harry Blackstone, Jnr shows his skills with a pack of playing cards.*

1 Ask your friend to write down a number from 100 to 999. They must choose a number in which the first and last digits are different by more than one. For example, 446 is fine, as the difference between 4 and 6 is 2. They can't choose 445 or 344, because the difference between the first and last digits is not more than one.

Top Tip!

Make sure that the piece of paper you use is thick enough so that your friend can't see that you have already written something on the other side.

446 reversed is 644

644
- 446

198

198 reversed is 891

198
+891

1089

2 Let's pretend that your friend chooses the number 446. Take 446 and turn it around so that you have 644. Then take away the smaller number 446 from the larger 644. This leaves 198.

3 Now reverse 198, which is 891. Add 198 and 891 together to get 1089. Now turn over the paper and show that you knew what the result would be! Surprisingly, it does not matter which number your friend starts with, the result will always be 1089.

Pick a picture

★★★

Ask your friend to think about just one object from a piece of cardboard containing more than 30 pictures. Then tell them which object they were thinking about!

Props needed...
* Cardboard
* Scissors

Preparation

• Photocopy these six charts onto thick paper or cardboard and cut out each one. There is one large card and five smaller ones.

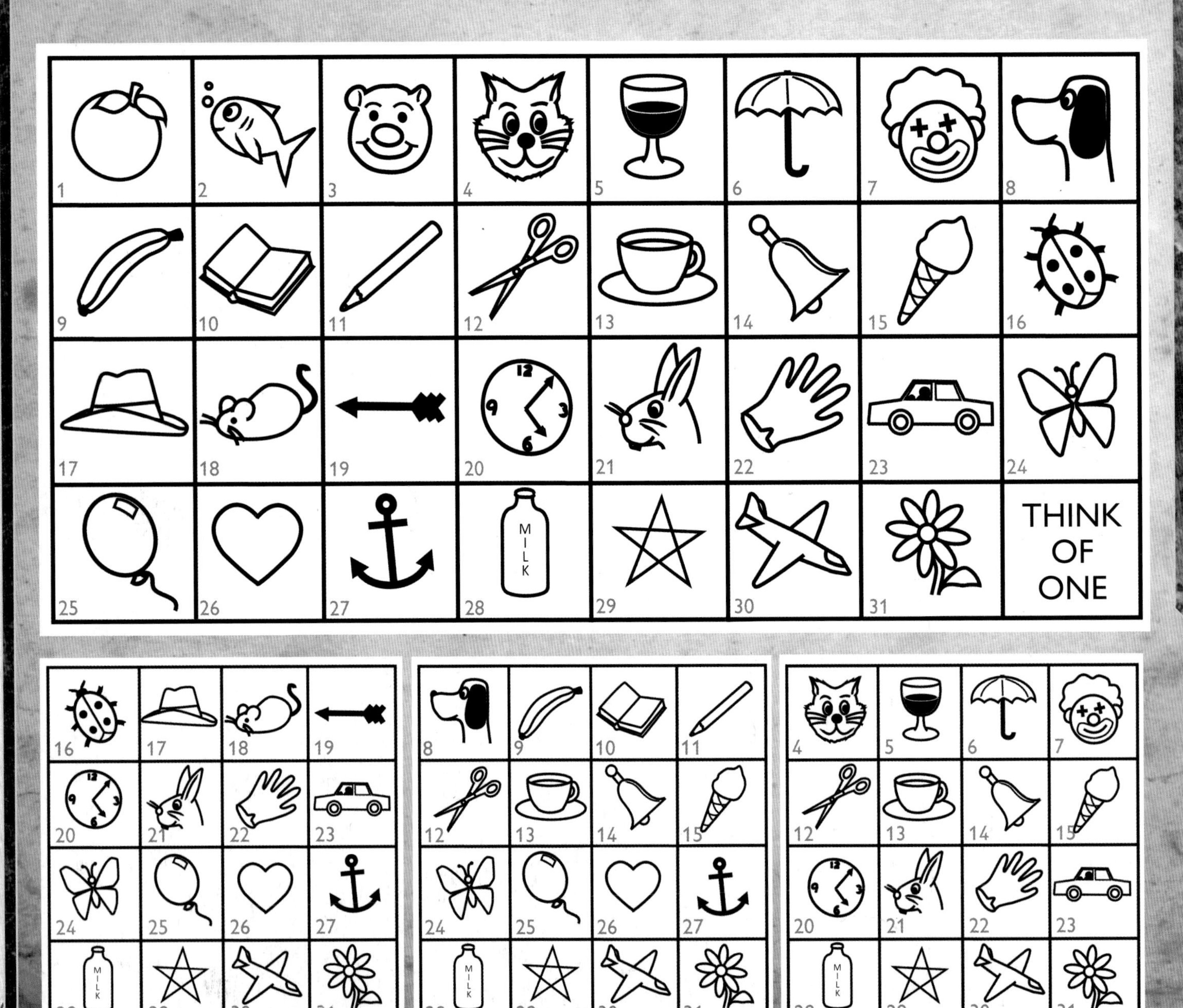

1 Show your friend the large card with 31 pictures on it. Ask your friend to think about just one of the objects.

2 Once your friend has picked one of the objects, give them the five smaller cards. Ask them to look at each smaller card carefully and give you back the cards that have a picture of the object that they are thinking about.

3 As soon as they have done this, you can tell which object they chose!

4 How? Easy! Add together the grey numbers that appear in the bottom left-hand picture of each of the smaller cards that your friend gives you back. Taking this total, look at the big chart and find the object that lies in the square with that number. This will be the object that your friend thought about. It works every time!

Magic 115 trick

★★★

Props needed...
* Pocket calculator

By using simple mathematics, and the magic number 115, you can tell a person the number that they are thinking about as well as their age!

1

It is best to do this trick with an adult whose age you do not know. Ask them to do the following:

– Enter their age into the calculator
– Multiply it by two
– Add five
– Multiply by 50
– Subtract 365
– Think of any number under 100 and add that to the total

The person then tells you the grand total, and you tell them their age and the number they had thought about! How can you possibly do this?

Age		44
x 2	=	88
+5	=	93
x 50	=	4650
-365	=	4285
+ 27	=	4312

2

Let's say that their age is 44 and the number they thought about was 27. The total they show you is 4312. This is where the magic number 115 is used! Secretly, add 115 to their total.

4312
+ 115

= 4427

3

The first two digits give us their age, and the second two give us the number they thought about. Easy!

To prove that it works every time, here are two more examples:

Age		56
x 2	=	112
+5	=	117
x 50	=	5850
-365	=	5485
+99	=	5584
+115	=	5699

A 56-year-old thinks of number 99.

Age		13
x 2	=	26
+5	=	31
x 50	=	1550
-365	=	1185
+24	=	1209
+115	=	1324

A 13-year-old thinks of number 24.

X-ray eyes

Kuda Bux (1906–1981) had an amazing act. While on stage, his eyes were covered with soft dough, aluminium foil, gauze and bandages, and his head wrapped in strips of cloth. He then amazed his audience by reading from books put in front of him. In August 1938 a 1-metre-deep pit was dug in a car park in New York. It was filled with charcoal and logs and set alight. Kuda Bux walked barefoot through the pit – twice!

▶ *How could Kuda Bux walk through the fiery pit? Afterwards his feet were not even warm!*

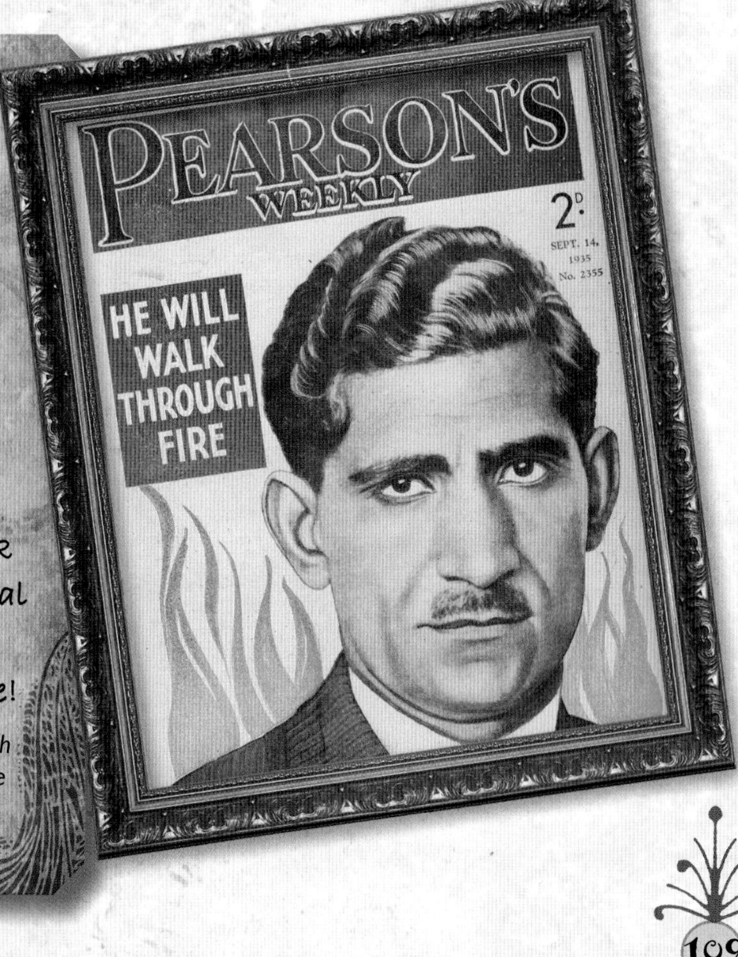

Passport to mystery

Your friend multiplies your passport number by a number they choose between 1 and 7. You, however, have already written down the total!

Props needed...

* Small notebook
* Long strip of paper
* Pencil
* Sticky tape
* Pocket calculator

Preparation

1. Write the number 142857 on the long slip of paper, with the digits spaced as shown.

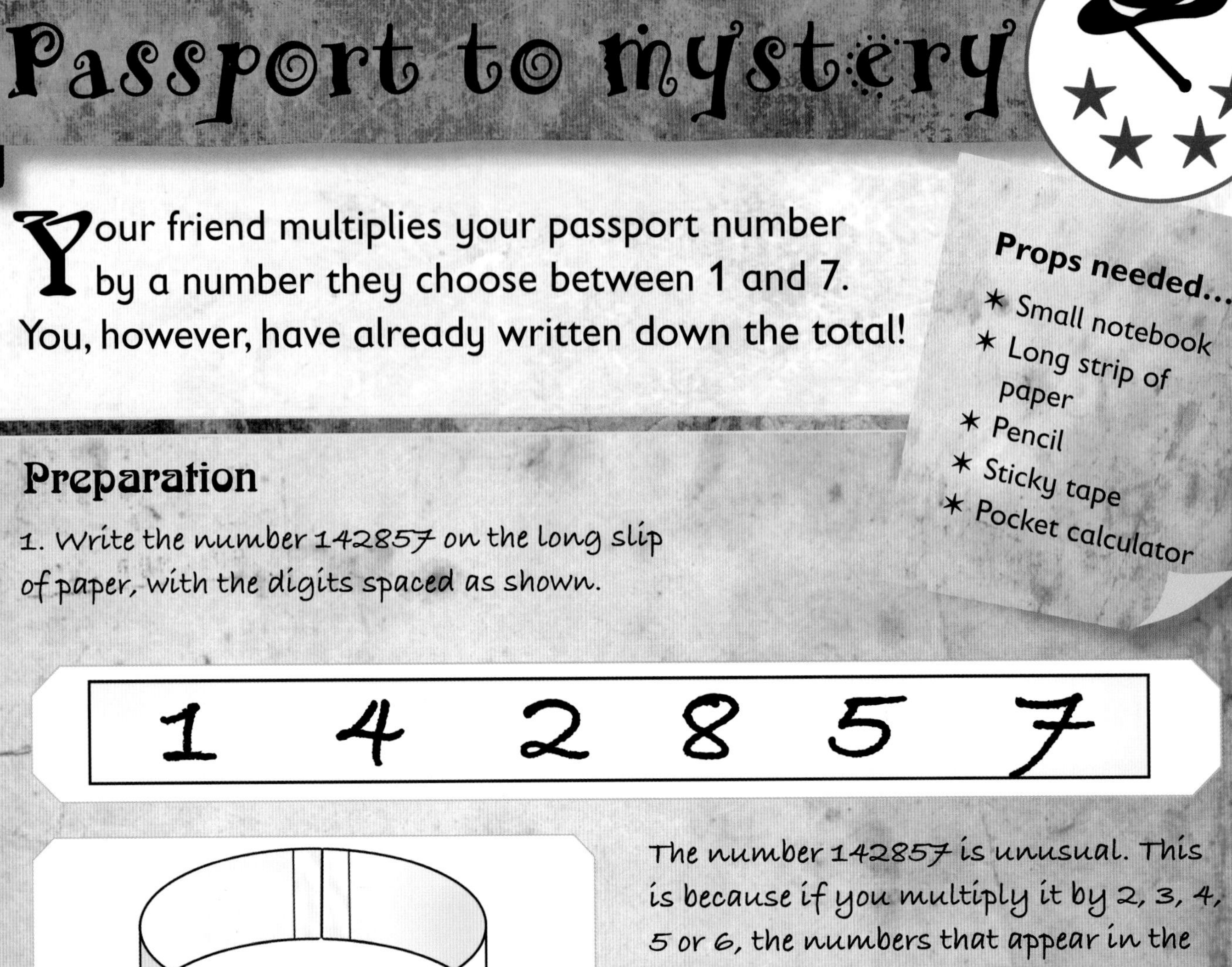

The number 142857 is unusual. This is because if you multiply it by 2, 3, 4, 5 or 6, the numbers that appear in the answer are the same. They can be read clockwise around the circle, starting at a different digit.

2. Join the two ends of the strip together with sticky tape. Flatten the circle and put it in your pocket.

3. Write 'Passport number 142857' in your notebook. You will pretend that this is your passport number. Put the notebook in your pocket.

142857 x 2 = 285714 – to read the answer, start at number 2

142857 x 3 = 428571 – to read the answer, start at number 4

142857 x 4 = 571428 – to read the answer, start at number 5

142857 x 5 = 714285 – to read the answer, start at number 7

142857 x 6 = 857142 – to read the answer, start at number 8

1 Start by giving the calculator to your friend. Then take the notebook and strip of paper out of your pocket.

2 Say that you will try an experiment with your passport number. Open the notebook and ask your friend to enter the number into the calculator as you read it out.

Your friend enters the number 142857 into the calculator.

4 Ask them to think of a number between 1 and 7 and say it out loud. Let's pretend they say '4'.

5 Ask your friend to multiply your passport number by 4.

6 As quickly as you can, tear the strip so that the number 5 becomes the first number on the left-hand side of your strip. Compare your strip to the calculator. The numbers are the same!

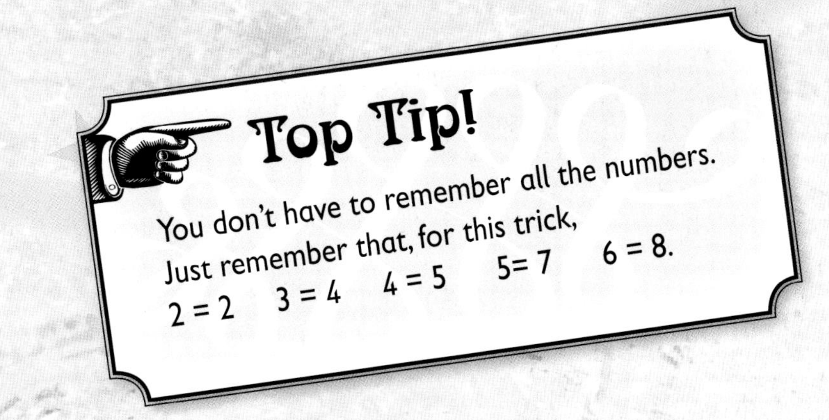

Top Tip!

You don't have to remember all the numbers. Just remember that, for this trick,

2 = 2 3 = 4 4 = 5 5= 7 6 = 8.

Piggy bank

This great trick shows how devious magicians can be! Your friend holds a number of coins hidden in their hands. You show that you know exactly how many coins they are holding.

Props needed...

* 200 coins
* Glass bowl
* Paper
* Pencil

Preparation

• Place the 200 coins into a clear glass bowl.

1 Ask your friend to grab a handful of coins from the glass bowl. Then, you grab a handful of coins. It is important that you pick up more coins than your friend.

2

Say to your friend, "In a moment we will turn our backs and count the number of coins we are holding. Please do not tell me how many coins you have – just remember the total." You also count your coins. Do not tell your friend how many coins you have.

3

Let's assume that you have picked up 33 coins. Subtract 3 from this total, giving you 30.

Top Tip!

You could have deducted any small number from your total at the start: say, 5. Then your statement would have been, "I have the same number of coins as you. I will have 5 over and enough left to make your total up to 28."

4

Say to your friend, "I'm going to make three statements, all of which are true."

1. "I will match the number of coins you have."
2. "I will have three coins extra."
3. "I will have enough coins left to take your total up to 30 coins."

"So, how many coins have you got?"

5

They say they have 19 coins. Now repeat each statement and give your friend the correct number of coins.

"I have the same number of coins as you." Put 19 coins back into the glass bowl from your coins.

"I will have three coins extra." Count three more coins back into the bowl.

"I will have enough coins left to take your total up to 30 coins." Count the remaining 11 coins back into the bowl to make 30 coins!

Him	You
19	33
+ 11	− 3
	30
= 30	− 19
	= 11

The 'Q' trick

Your friend silently looks at a playing card, which is somewhere in a spread of cards. You do not know which card this is, but you still find it!

Props needed...

* Pack of playing cards

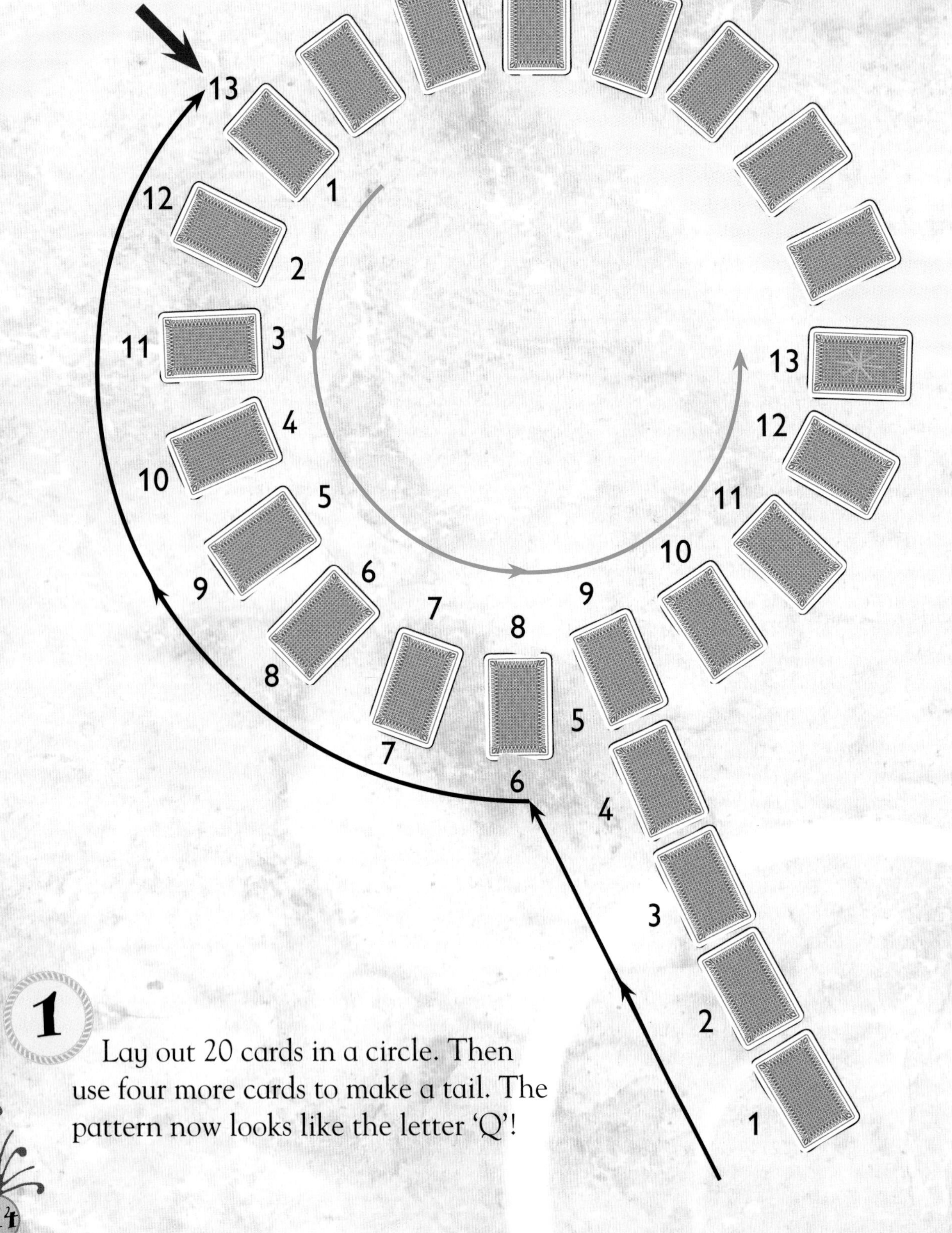

1

Lay out 20 cards in a circle. Then use four more cards to make a tail. The pattern now looks like the letter 'Q'!

2

Ask your friend to think of a number between 5 and 20. Starting with card 1 at the end of the tail, they should then silently count the cards until they reach the number they are thinking about. They must move around the circle in a clockwise direction. In other words, using the numbers on the outside of the circle in the diagram.

3

When they reach the card with the number they were thinking about, they should make this card the new card 1. If they were thinking of the number 13, card 13 is now the new card 1 – this is marked with a red arrow in the diagram. Tell them again that they must do all this silently.

4

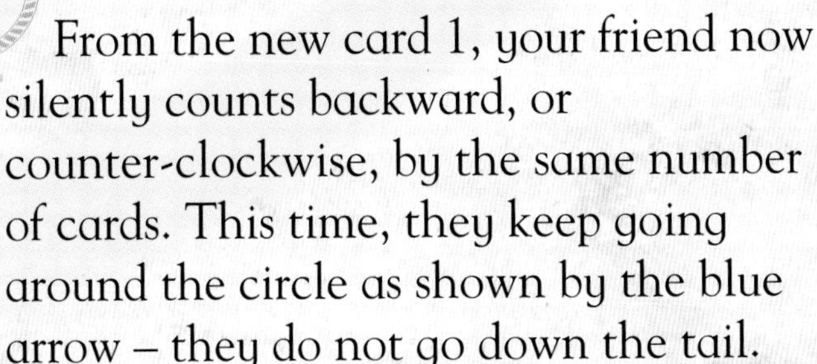

From the new card 1, your friend now silently counts backward, or counter-clockwise, by the same number of cards. This time, they keep going around the circle as shown by the blue arrow – they do not go down the tail. Tell them that, when they reach the new card, they must look at and think about the card. They should not tell you what the card is.

5

Now pass your hand over all the cards as if trying to pick up a vibration from them. Finally, you pick up the correct card and hand it to your friend!

How do you do this? The answer lies in the tail of the Q. There are five cards in the tail, so your friend's card will be the fifth card counting counterclockwise from the top of the tail. It does not matter which number they think about; they will always arrive at the same position. Try it for yourself and see!

Top Tip!

If you want to repeat the trick, just put a few more cards in the tail. Your friend's final position will then be slightly different.

Matching halves

Your friend tells you how to divide up five playing cards that you have cut in half. You manage to match up the half-cards, even though they are placed face down on the table.

Props needed...

* Any five playing cards from an old pack

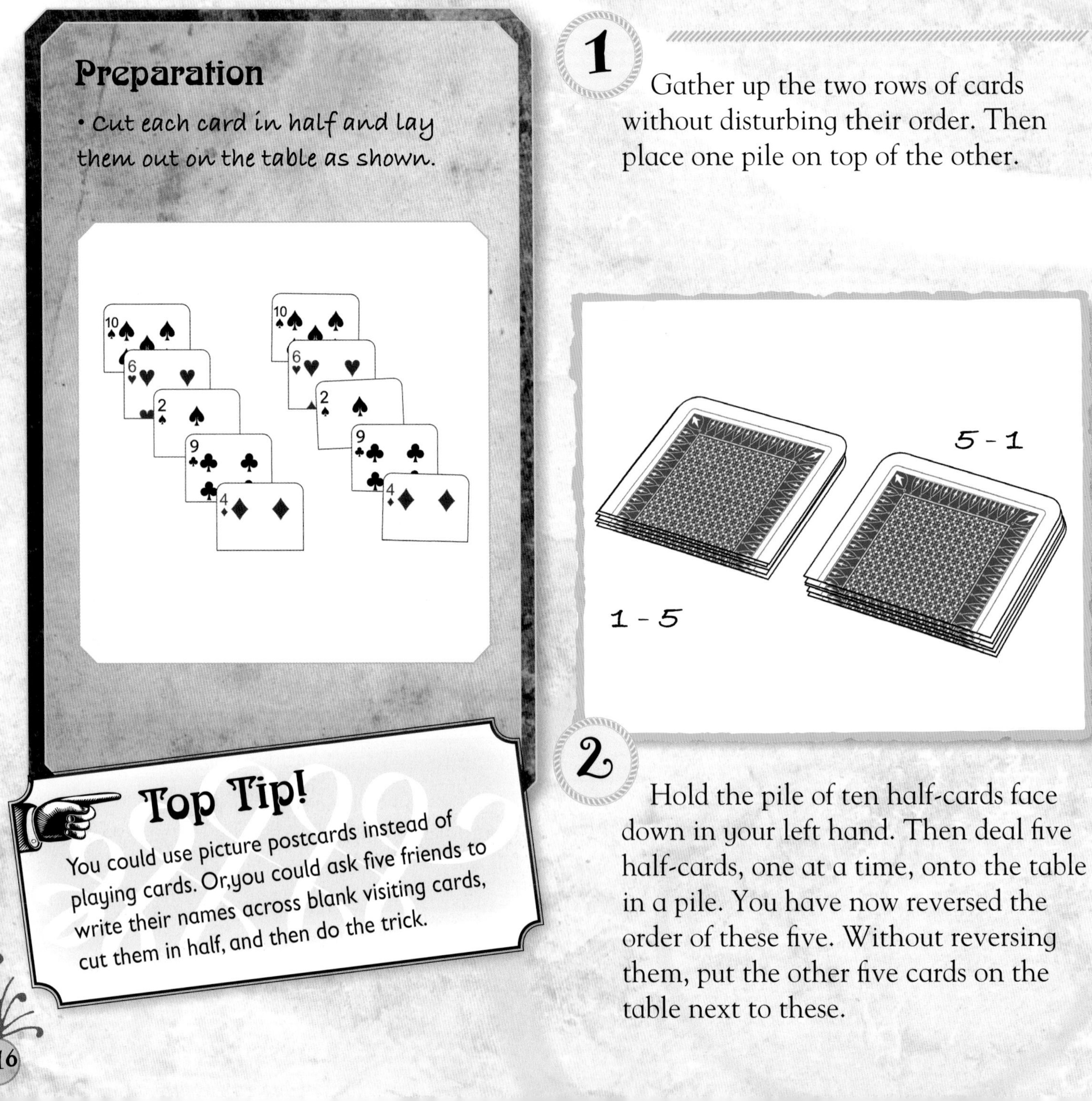

Preparation

• Cut each card in half and lay them out on the table as shown.

1 Gather up the two rows of cards without disturbing their order. Then place one pile on top of the other.

2 Hold the pile of ten half-cards face down in your left hand. Then deal five half-cards, one at a time, onto the table in a pile. You have now reversed the order of these five. Without reversing them, put the other five cards on the table next to these.

Top Tip!

You could use picture postcards instead of playing cards. Or,you could ask five friends to write their names across blank visiting cards, cut them in half, and then do the trick.

3

Say to your friend, "This trick uses the phrase 'Last Two Cards Match'. I am going to spell out the phrase 'Last Two Cards Match' using these pieces of card. You are going to tell me exactly what to do and you must make sure that I obey all your instructions. Let's start."

4

"Which of the two piles would you like me to start with?" When your friend points to a pile, you pick it up. "Our first word is 'Last'. I remove one half-card from the top of this pile and take it to the bottom of the pile to represent the letter 'L'." While you are talking, make this move.

5

"Now we must move a half-card for the next letter, 'A'. Shall I use the pile that I'm holding or the other pile?" If your friend says the pile that you are holding, just move a card, as before. Use the other pile if they ask for this. Do the same for the letters 'S' and 'T', obeying your friend's instructions. Now take the top card from each pile and place both on one side, without showing their faces.

6

Do the same for the words 'Two', 'Cards' and 'Match'. Remember to put aside the next two top half-cards when you finish spelling each word. You are now left with two half-cards.

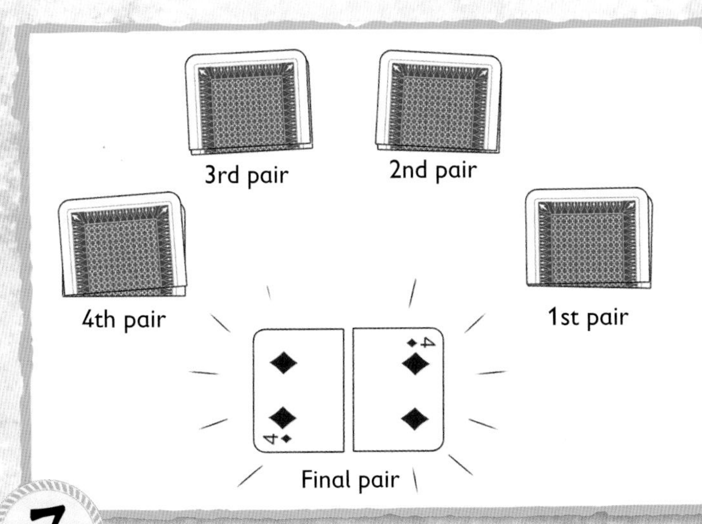

7

Turn them over to show that the last two cards do match! Your friend will think the trick is over, but you have a surprise for them.

8

Turn the other four sets of pairs face up. Wow – they all match up too!

Pieces of eight

Throw eight small objects into a box. Ask your friend to think of one, without telling you what it is. Then take them out, one by one, until you know you are holding the one your friend chose!

Preparation

- Each of the objects that you use has a different number of letters in its name. You can use other items, but make sure they have the right number of letters.

chewing gum	10 letters
safety pin	9 letters
bracelet	8 letters
battery	7 letters
button	6 letters
match	5 letters
ring	4 letters
key	3 letters

- Make sure the objects are small enough for each to be hidden in a clenched hand.

- Remember how many letters there are in the name of each object.

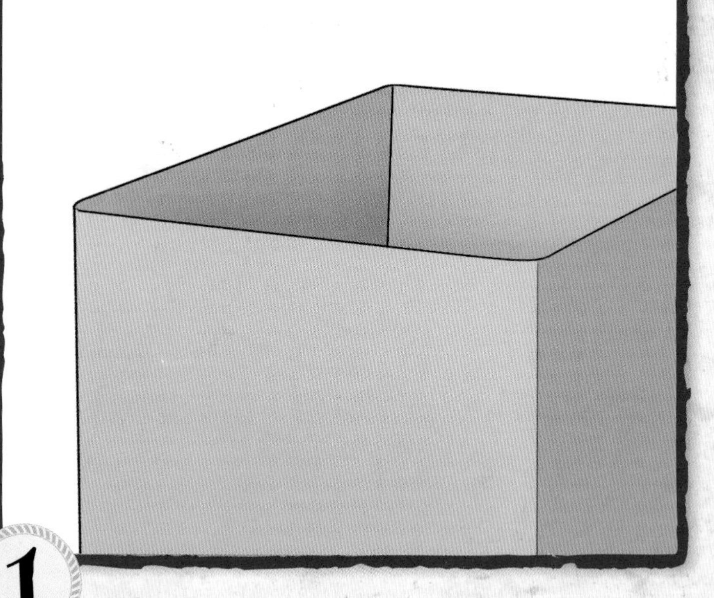

1 Put all eight objects on the table together with the box. Pick up the objects in any order and put them in the box. As you do so, name each one out loud. For example, say "match", "bracelet", and so on.

2 Ask a friend to look into the box. They should silently choose one of the objects and think about it.

3 Explain that you will now lift objects out of the box, one at a time. The object will be hidden in your hand. Each time you take an object out, your friend must silently think about one letter of the name of their chosen object. When they reach the last letter of the name, they must say, "Stop."

4 Put your hand in the box and take out any object, hidden in your clenched hand. Wait a few seconds, then put the object back in the box. Then take out another one.

5 Put the object back into the box after a few seconds. This time, take out the key. If your friend is thinking of the key (three letters), they will now shout, "Stop!" Ask them to tell you which object they were thinking about. They say, "The key". You open your hand and, to their amazement, there is the key!

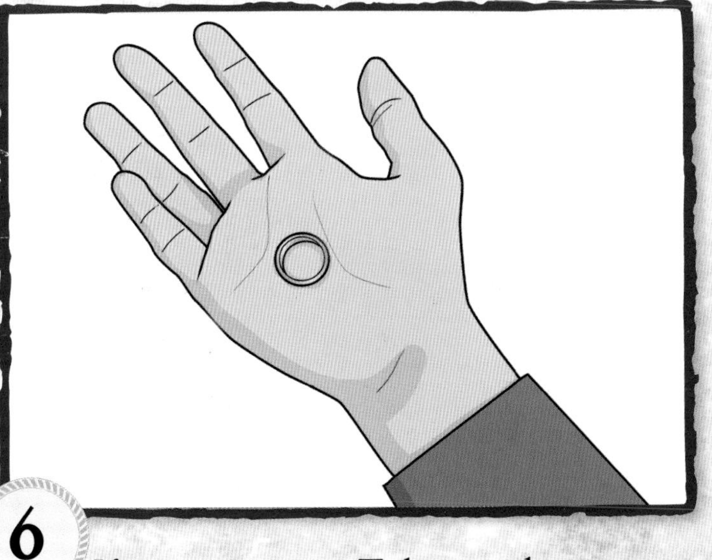

6 If not, continue. Take out the ring (four letters). If they are thinking of the ring, they will shout, "Stop!" – there is the ring in your hand!

7 Continue taking out the object with the next largest number of letters in its name. Do this until your friend shouts, "Stop." Whenever you open your hand, the correct object will be in it!

Maths puzzle

How can you get two different answers for the same sum? It depends on how you approach the problem!

1. Three friends reach a hotel late at night, but only one room is available. They decide to share the room.

2. The room costs £30 for the night, so each person agrees to pay £10.

3. They go up to the room. After a while, there is a knock on the door. It is the hotel porter, who tells them that, as it is Wednesday night, the room is only £25, not £30. The porter gives them back £5.

4. The friends are so impressed with the honesty of the porter that they give him a £2 tip and keep £1 each.

These are the sums.

	Friend one	Friend two	Friend three
Cost of room	£10	£10	£10
Refund	£1	£1	£1
Total cost each	£9	£9	£9

The tip to the porter was £2

So that is £9 + £9 + £9 + £2, which is £29!

What has happened to the other £1? Let's start again!

1. With the £5 refund, the friends paid £25 for the room, not £30.

2. So it cost each friend one third of £25, which is £8.33.

3. They decided to tip the porter £2 and each keep £1.

4. The £5 was their money in the first place and has got nothing to do with the cost of the room. Therefore, there was no vanishing £1!